THROUGH THE EYE OF A NEEDLE

The Doctrine of Nonaccumulation

Roger Hertzler

Benchmark Press
Shippensburg, Pennsylvania
2008

Through the Eye of a Needle: The Doctrine of Nonaccumulation.
Revised edition.
© 2008 by Roger Hertzler. All rights reserved.
Benchmark Press, Shippensburg, Pa.

ISBN: 978-0-924722-20-2

First printing 2007.
Second printing 2008.

Distributed by:
Scroll Publishing
P.O. Box 122
Amberson, PA 17210
(717) 349-7033
www.scrollpublishing.com

Cover Design – Heather Browne

Printed in the United States of America.

CONTENTS

INTRODUCTION

The teaching you are about to read is radical. At least it will seem radical to you if you have never heard this teaching before. It seemed extremely radical to me the first time I heard it.

However, being radical was not new to me. Growing up in a conservative Anabaptist church, I had always been taught that as Christians, it was our duty to obey the commands of Christ even if doing so made us stick out from the people around us. We were taught especially that Christ's Sermon on the Mount was meant to be practiced today, and not to be put on hold until some future era. This sermon was the basis for our distinctive teachings about divorce and remarriage, nonswearing of oaths, and nonresistance. We were not afraid to stand out from the people around us, both Christians and non-Christians alike, on these issues. This belief in the necessity of obedience for salvation and the place of the Sermon on the Mount in our present day lives is the foundation for believing in the doctrine of nonaccumulation.

If, however, you are a Christian who believes that salvation is by "faith alone," and that obedience is not a necessary part of it, please allow yourself to be challenged by skipping forward and reading chapter 4: Thoughts on Interpreting Scripture. Perhaps you won't change your mind after reading this one chapter. But I ask you at least to open the door of your heart, especially where God's Word is quoted, and to examine the things you have always believed to be true. And, as in every controversy, "let God be true, but every man a liar."

A servant of Jesus,
Roger Hertzler

1

WHAT IS A DOCTRINE?

In 1928, Daniel Kauffman compiled a book entitled *Doctrines of the Bible.* In this volume, he identified and expounded on roughly 62 different Bible "doctrines" such as the Trinity, the Atonement, Baptism, Nonconformity, Nonresistance, and the Second Coming of Christ.

Some might question the purpose for such a book. Why can't we just read the Bible and believe what it says? Why do we have to take broad Biblical truths and distill them into these neat little packages that we call "doctrines"?

This question is a valid one. The Christian church certainly has spent an enormous amount of energy through the centuries developing, articulating, and defending a huge variety of doctrines, both true and false. And much of this energy, no doubt, would appear to God as an utter waste of time and resources.

On the other hand, to identify a particular set of ideas as a doctrine does provide several important services. First, it provides us with a "line in the sand" that individuals or churches can examine and then ask themselves this question: "Do we or don't we accept this doctrine as a true Bible doctrine?" The answer to this question, in turn, gives us a concise way to communicate our beliefs to others. (It is far easier to say, for instance, "We believe in the doctrine of the Trinity" than it is to give a detailed explanation of exactly what the doctrine of the Trinity teaches.)

If a doctrine has been defined well, the decision to accept or reject it becomes a simple "yes or no" question. The answer should be either yes, we accept it as a true doctrine, or no, we reject it as a false doctrine. There shouldn't be much room for saying, "Well, I accept part of it," or "Well, there's some truth to it, but there needs to be some balance." These statements *may* be appropriate when it comes to the practical applications of the doctrine. But they are not valid responses to the question of whether we accept the doctrine itself as a true doctrine.

The fact that two different individuals may agree to embrace a particular doctrine as true does not mean that they will practice this doctrine in exactly the same way. Different people often are at different places *practically* despite their agreement with one another *doctrinally*. These differences, however, ought never to be used as a basis for accepting or rejecting the doctrine itself.

Second, defining a set of beliefs as a doctrine provides a sort of theological guardrail against future apostasy. This does not mean that the provided guardrail cannot be crossed. It simply means that future generations will be slower to drop a doctrine officially accepted by a church body than to discard a set of beliefs that has never been defined in this way.

The purpose of this book, then, is threefold. First, it aims to define the doctrine of nonaccumulation, and thus draw that "line in the sand" that we as Christians or groups of Christians can examine and then decide: Do we accept this doctrine as a true doctrine? Or do we reject it as a false doctrine?

Second, for those of you who until now have not accepted this doctrine as true, I want an opportunity to influence you to do so. At a minimum, I want to ask whether you would be willing to consider the possibility that the doctrine of nonaccumulation *might* be true, and to give yourself to the study of God's Word to discover the truth about this question.

Third, for those of you who have accepted it as a true doctrine, I want to strengthen you in that belief and perhaps provide you with a few suggestions regarding its practical application.

"So you're trying to introduce a new doctrine to us?" I can hear some of you asking.

The answer is no. The doctrine of nonaccumulation is not a new doctrine at all, not by any stretch of the imagination. It is a doctrine as old as Christianity itself. However, it is a doctrine that has been lost to most of today's Christians, including those who would call themselves conservative. In the future, will these Christians continue to let go of Bible doctrines they have previously held? Or will they choose to recover this doctrine that has been lost? My fear is that, in the long run, it must be one or the other.

2

WHAT IS THE DOCTRINE OF NONACCUMULATION?

A teacher at a Bible school for young people stands up and announces, "In our class on Christian Stewardship today we are going to look specifically at the subject of financial management and some Biblical principles about how we are to handle money." He then goes on to teach about long-range planning, especially emphasizing the benefits of disciplining ourselves to put at least a small amount of money each month into savings.

He demonstrates mathematically the tremendous power of compound interest, especially for someone who starts saving at a young age. "If at age 20 you would put $10,000 in an investment that earns an average annual interest rate of 8%, by the age of 65 this investment will have grown to about $320,000. And this is true even if you don't add anything more to it!

"What about those of you who don't have $10,000 to invest at age 20? Well, you could instead decide to set aside just $60 per month—$2 per day—and if put into this same investment, it too will have grown to about $320,000 by the time you reach age 65."

Next, the teacher gives the illustration of two families: the "Bigs" and the "Smalls." Both couples start out with similar incomes and similar personal needs. Both couples have $1,000 to spend on housing each month. The Bigs' first house is an expensive one with a mortgage payment of $1,000 per month for 30 years. The Smalls decide to start out smaller, with lower monthly payments, and to put the difference into savings. Several years later they trade up to a house equal in size to that

4

of the Bigs, and continue to make payments at $1,000 per month. The end result is that by the time the Bigs get their house paid for, the Smalls have not only paid for their house, but also have built up a savings account worth several hundred thousand dollars.

The students, noticeably impressed, take part in the ensuing class discussion about how a person can, by a little hard work and consistent self-discipline, build up for himself a nice nest egg for the future. This money then will be available to care for his personal needs, to give to his church, or to pass on to his children.

Another teacher at a different Bible school makes this statement: "When Jesus gave the command 'Lay not up for yourselves treasures on earth', He literally meant that as His followers, we are not to accumulate unused wealth on this earth." This teacher then goes on to bring other Scriptures into the discussion, including the *reasons* Christ has forbidden us to accumulate wealth and the *consequences* we'll face if we do it anyway.

What is the reason for such a stark contradiction between these two messages, coming from two men who would agree with each other on so many other Bible principles?

The answer lies in the difference between their views on one particular Bible doctrine: the doctrine of nonaccumulation. The second teacher accepts this doctrine as a true doctrine. The first teacher does not.

So what is the doctrine of nonaccumulation? Quite simply, it is the doctrine stating that Jesus forbids His people to accumulate wealth on this earth, but rather commands them to distribute those possessions they do not currently need for the needs of others and for spreading the gospel.

Or to condense it into a few words, this doctrine says that Jesus commands us to distribute rather than accumulate earthly wealth.

That, in a nutshell, is the definition for the doctrine of nonaccumulation. This definition, by itself, does not address any of the questions about *how* or *to what extent* we are to put this doctrine into practice. All such questions ("May we do this?" or "Must we do that?" or "What about this situation?") must, for now, simply be left hanging.

The primary question we address at this point, rather, is simply this: Is this doctrine, as stated, a true doctrine or a false doctrine? It has to be one or the other. It cannot be both. This book's purpose is to help you, the reader, find the answer to this question.

3

STOP . . . CONSIDER!

Perhaps after reading the definition of this doctrine in chapter 2, you are ready to throw this book aside and reject it as a bunch of nonsense. "Of course I don't believe such a doctrine," you might be thinking. "I've never heard it taught in my church, so it must be just another new heresy coming down the pike. I'll take my stand against this doctrine just as I would against any other false doctrine."

Or perhaps you have taken a quick mental inventory of what it would cost you personally to accept this doctrine as true. And you've decided that it would be easier to reject this doctrine as false from the outset than to risk investigating it further.

But before you throw this book down in disgust, please consider what it has cost other people to reject a doctrine before they have given it a fair hearing.

Consider some of the beliefs you espouse that others do not. You believe, for instance, that the only way to God is through a man named Jesus of Nazareth. To someone else, however, this view may seem egotistical and narrow-minded. Yet what is the cost to that person if he throws the idea away without examining the evidence for it?

Or, maybe you could look at some of the finer points of your Christian faith. Perhaps you believe in the doctrine of nonresistance, and that a Christian cannot take part in war if he is to be obedient to Jesus. Consider, however, how hard it would be for your patriotic neighbor to accept this idea. He has been taught all his life about the importance of patriotism and that God expects us to support and defend our country. Consider especially how hard this would be for him to accept if he is actually in the military himself, and has only a few years left until he can receive full retirement benefits. Yet what is the cost to him if he rejects this doctrine on that basis?

Or, if you have accepted Jesus' teaching against divorce and remarriage, you would rightly conclude that anyone who wants to join your church would also need to accept this doctrine as true. Yet think of what this would mean to someone who is actually in a divorce and remarriage situation. (It's no wonder that in today's society most Christians reject this idea as being too radical.) Yet what is the cost to those who do reject it?

Consider also the story of the rich young ruler. This man once stood at a crossroads similar to the one you may be standing at now. In the end, he rejected the command of Jesus to "sell and give." I don't know what all his reasoning was. Perhaps he thought that this really wasn't God who was giving this command. Perhaps he thought that he would eventually find some less costly way to obtain eternal life. Perhaps he even recognized that he was giving up his opportunity for salvation, but decided it was worth it if he could keep his riches. (For further discussion on this story, please read the chapter in this book entitled "The Real Mistake of the Rich Young Ruler.") Whatever his reasoning was, it caused him to reject the very Son of God. And how much did this rejection really cost him in the long run?

Finally, consider whether there is any real danger in reading on. Suppose you come away from this book convinced that the doctrine of nonaccumulation is a true doctrine. If so, it is a gift to you from One Whose love for you is infinite! It has been given for your benefit, not for your harm. Is that anything to be afraid of? If, on the other hand, this doctrine does not stand the test of Scripture, you can just reject it and go on with your life.

I therefore urge you to continue reading this book to the end. Not to get a message from a mere human such as me, but rather to consider whether God Himself has a message for you, a message that you may never have considered before.

If nothing else, at least read the Scriptures contained in this book (we at least have to recognize that they come from God). I would guess that some of the verses mentioned in this book are verses that you never even realized were in the Bible. (At least that's how it was for me with these verses.) And we certainly can't say we've given honest consideration to this doctrine unless we've looked at all the Scriptures that pertain to it.

4

THOUGHTS ON
INTERPRETING SCRIPTURE

If we are going to be looking into God's Word for answers in this study, it seems we ought to establish from the outset some basic principles on how to interpret what we read. So here are a few of the principles I intend to follow, to the best of my ability.

1. To accept as the correct interpretation *the one that is the most literal*, when taken in the context of all the other New Testament verses that pertain to it.

2. To begin with the very *words of Jesus* as the foundation for our study. We will move next to the remainder of the New Testament, which, if interpreted correctly, will build upon, but never contradict, the words of Jesus Christ.

3. To recognize the *differences in dispensation* between the Old Testament and the New Testament, and that Jesus clearly overruled some of the commands in the Old Testament by some of the commands He gave us in the New Testament.

4. To recognize that *obedience to Christ* is a necessary part of a saving relationship with Him. If we do not abide in Christ in an obedient, loving, believing relationship with Him, the Father will cut us off from the vine, and we will lose our salvation.

5. To recognize that Christ's *Sermon on the Mount* is meant to be lived out by us in this day and age, and is not to be set aside for some future time.

In my own religious background (conservative Anabaptist), we have always believed in these basic principles. We were taught that following the Sermon on the Mount was an integral part of following Jesus. We were taught that obedience was necessary, not optional, if we were to call ourselves Christians. And we were faithfully warned about the danger of falling away even after having begun the Christian life.

Those of us who were taught these things all our lives in some respects have an advantage as we begin this study. For us, the foundation has already been laid for accepting this doctrine as true. We already believe in Jesus as the only begotten Son of God. We already believe that obeying Him is necessary. And we already believe that the Sermon on the Mount is meant for us to put into practice today.

If, however, you are a Christian who does not believe in any or all of the aforementioned principles, may I challenge you to examine your beliefs in light of the following Scriptures?

First, what is the role of obedience to Christ in our salvation? (Is obedience to Him really necessary, or is salvation simply a matter of "believing" in Him without any real commitment to obey Him?)

Ye are my friends, if ye do whatsoever I command you (Jn. 15:14).

And hereby we do know that we know him, if we keep his commandments (1 Jn. 2:3).

If ye love me, keep my commandments (Jn. 14:15).

Blessed are they that do his commandments, that they may have right to the tree of life, and may enter in through the gates into the city (Rev. 22:14).

If ye keep my commandments, ye shall abide in my love; even as I have kept my Father's commandments, and abide in his love (Jn. 15:10).

Therefore whosoever heareth these sayings of mine, and doeth them, I will liken him unto a wise man, which built his house upon a rock (Mt. 7:24).

Second, what is the condition of those who do not obey Jesus?

And why call ye me, Lord, Lord, and do not the things which I say? (Lk. 6:46).

Not every one that saith unto me, Lord, Lord, shall enter into the kingdom of heaven; but he that doeth the will of my Father which is in heaven (Mt. 7:21).

He that saith, I know him, and keepeth not his commandments, is a liar, and the truth is not in him (1 Jn. 2:4).

Every branch in me that beareth not fruit he taketh away (Jn. 15:2).

In flaming fire taking vengeance on them that know not God, and that obey not the gospel of our Lord Jesus Christ (2 Thess. 1:8).

And every one that heareth these sayings of mine, and doeth them not, shall be likened unto a foolish man, which built his house upon the sand (Mt. 7:26).

Third, if obedience is necessary, then which of Jesus' commands are we supposed to obey? This question at first may seem a little silly. Once we have determined that obedience to Christ is necessary, then it only makes sense to say that we are required to obey all of His commands. Correct?

Well, let's try this. One of the commands of Jesus was "Go wash in the pool of Siloam." Are we supposed to obey that command?

No, obviously not. Therefore, it must not be right to say that we have to obey "all" the commands of Christ. Does that mean, then, that we get to pick and choose which commands we want to obey? Again, the answer is no. So what is the right way to know which commands apply to us?

The answer to this question lies in Jesus' words in the Great Commission, found in Matthew 28.

> Teaching them to observe all things *whatsoever I have commanded you*: and lo, I am with you alway, even unto the end of the world (Mt. 28:20).*

Jesus was talking to His disciples in these verses, and in these five words, "whatsoever I have commanded you," He gives the key to knowing which commands we are expected to keep: namely, those commands that He gave to His disciples. If a particular command was given to His disciples (in a teaching context), it was meant for us as well. If, on the other hand, the command was given to some other individual, we are generally not required to obey it.

This is the basis for believing that the Sermon on the Mount is for us to put into practice today. At the beginning of Matthew 5, although a multitude was present, it is clearly stated that Jesus was speaking to His disciples. This entire sermon, therefore, fits clearly within the "whatsoever I have commanded you" given in Matthew 28:20.

---

*Unless otherwise noted, all italics in quoted material have been added by the author.

To summarize, this study is built upon the belief that we are to obey the commands Christ gave to His disciples, including the Sermon on the Mount, if we want to call ourselves His people.

5

THE FIRST MAIN PILLAR

T wo commands of Jesus serve as the primary pillars on which this doctrine of nonaccumulation is built. The first is found in the Sermon on the Mount, in the sixth chapter of Matthew. Here, Jesus gives this command:

Lay not up for yourselves treasures on earth (Mt. 6:19).

I had always heard Matthew 6:19 explained to mean that Jesus is telling us what kind of *attitude* we are to have about our possessions, not necessarily what we are to *do* with them. Because Jesus uses the word "treasures" in this passage, He is speaking only about those possessions that we "treasure" in our heart.

A simple word study, however, will show that this is not the case. The word Jesus uses that has been translated as *treasure* simply means "wealth." The words *lay up* simply mean to "store up," or "to accumulate." The most literal interpretation of this verse, therefore, is that Jesus forbids His followers to accumulate wealth on this earth.

But, we might ask, what exactly does it mean to accumulate wealth? If I have a thousand dollars in the bank, am I guilty of accumulating wealth? How about a hundred dollars? Or ten dollars?

Jesus does not give us many specifics about putting this command into practice. But He does give us one example of someone who violated this command. This is found in the parable of the rich fool in Luke 12:16–20.

We all have heard many times this story of the rich farmer, about how he had made a large profit farming, about how he decided to tear down his barns and build greater, and about how God rebuked him and told him that he would die that very night. And we have heard many explanations about this parable and what the mistake was of this man that God called a "fool." Some have said that his mistake was that he forgot to pray and ask God's advice before making plans for the future. Others have said that his mistake was pride, or laziness, or self-sufficiency, or his failure to accept Christ.

Thankfully, we do not have to speculate about what this man's mistake was, because with this particular parable, Jesus provides us with the luxury of an explanation about what it meant. It is found in verse 21, and it begins with the words "so is he."

If Jesus had said, "so is he who forgets to seek counsel from God," or "so is he who is proud," or "so is he who fails to believe in Me," then we would have this as our answer about the meaning of this parable. But Jesus doesn't say any of these things. Instead, he says:

So is he that layeth up treasure for himself (Lk. 12:21).

So this man's actions clearly fit into the category of "laying up treasures" in violation of the prohibition Jesus gave in Matthew 6:19. Note that Jesus does not condemn this man for *earning* the profits (nor, specifically, for owning the assets necessary to make the profits). It was the *laying up* of these profits on this earth that brought him into condemnation.

This man had earned an income, paid his expenses, and converted the remainder into commodities that could have been given to those in need. But he chose instead to store them up indefinitely for himself. In doing so, he proved that he loved himself more than he loved others. He proved that his heart was here on earth, with his treasures, rather than in Heaven with God. And he missed forever the opportunity to invest in something that could never have been taken from him.

———————————

There are some very natural questions that will tend to arise if we decide that this command of Jesus (not to store up wealth on earth) was meant to be taken literally: "What if we have a large medical bill?" "What if I lose my job?" "What if I become disabled?"

Jesus anticipated that such questions would arise, and therefore gives us this instruction:

> Therefore take no thought saying, What shall we eat? or What shall we drink? or Wherewithal shall we be clothed? (For after all these things do the Gentiles seek) (Mt. 6:31-32).

In other words, Jesus says, "I forbid you to ask this kind of question." Why?

> For your heavenly Father knoweth that ye have need of all these things (Mt. 6:32).

The response of true faith is first to obey and then to leave the consequences in the hands of our all-loving, all-powerful Creator.

———————————

The idea that the word "treasures" refers only to those possessions that we treasure flies in the face of another statement Jesus made. Whereas this idea says we need to look first at our *heart* to determine whether our possessions are our *treasure* or not, Jesus says exactly the opposite.

For where your treasure is, there will your heart be also (Mt. 6:21).

In other words, says Jesus, look first at your treasure (where you are making your investments), and that will tell you where your heart is. Don't try to look first at your heart. It's too deceitful, and probably won't give you an honest answer anyway. Look instead at your possessions, and then you will know where your heart is.

Many of us have tried to deny that this statement applies to us. We say that although we own an abundance of material things, our heart is not really in our possessions. Yet when the test actually comes, and we are faced with giving up those possessions, one by one we all prove that our heart actually was in them.

For example, there are many people who have a large savings account or who own a number of investment properties. When asked about the purpose for owning these assets, they say it is so that they can take care of themselves in case of a calamity such as a large medical bill. When that large medical bill comes, however, these same people lament sadly that they had to "dip into savings" or "sell off property" to pay the bill, as though it were some sort of tremendous hardship to do so.

———————————————

To summarize, it seems clear that Jesus' command in Matthew 6:19 ("lay not up") is a command not to accumulate wealth on this earth. It does not appear that our Lord is placing limits on the amount of money we *earn*. Rather, he is restricting what we do with that money once we have earned it. Specifically, He is forbidding us to *accumulate* it, to *invest* it, to *store it up* here on this earth.

Perhaps, however, you will respond to this suggestion in much the same way that others have done: "But I just don't believe that is what he is saying."

If that is your response, then I thank you for being honest. But before you ride off into the sunset with this as your opinion, please allow me to ask you two simple questions.

First, if Jesus doesn't really mean "don't accumulate," then what exactly does He mean by this command? What exactly is it that he is telling us not to do?

Second, if Jesus would have wanted to forbid the accumulation of earthly wealth, how else could he have said it? What words could he have used to make Himself more clear?

6

THE SECOND MAIN PILLAR

I n this chapter, we look at the second of the two primary commands on which the doctrine of nonaccumulation is built. But before I give you the reference for this verse, please take a little test regarding your Bible knowledge.

In chapter 4 we discussed how we are to know which of Jesus commands are for us to obey today. We answered, based on the authority of Matthew 28:20, that they consist of those commands that Jesus gave (in a teaching context) *to His disciples*. Therefore, we could divide all of Jesus' commands into two categories: those he gave to His disciples (category 1 commands) and those he gave to other people (category 2 commands). Category 1 commands, such as those given in the Sermon on the Mount, are binding on us today. Category 2 commands, such as those given to the blind man or to the woman at the well, do not (necessarily) apply to us today.

Here, then, is the test. When I quote the words of a particular command of Christ, try to identify it as a category 1 or category 2 command without looking it up. Ready? Here's the command:

Sell your possessions and give to the poor.

Was your answer "category 1" or "category 2"?

If you are like most Christians, you said that this is a category 2 command. You recognized it immediately as the command given to the rich young ruler. Because, then, it was given to someone other than Jesus' disciples, it must not apply to us today. Correct?

Actually, wrong. You see, I was not quoting from the story of the rich young ruler (found in Luke 18, Matthew 19, and

Mark 10). Rather, this quote comes from Luke 12:33, and Jesus was speaking to none other than to *His disciples!*

This command reads, depending on which translation you use, as follows:

Sell that ye have, and give alms (KJV).
Sell your possessions and give to the poor (NIV).
Sell your possessions and give to charity (NASB).

Whether we like this command or not, there it is, in the same Bible you've been carrying to church with you every week. And if you are like many Christians I've talked to, this may well be the first time you've really noticed this command.

Whatever it is that Jesus means by this command, we can know for sure that it was given to us by God Almighty. Whatever it is that He means, it is just as much a command as "Love your enemies" or "Swear not at all." Whatever it is that He means, disobedience to this command is just as much disobedience as adultery or murder. Whatever it is that He means, Christ's question to those who ignore this command is, "Why call ye me Lord, Lord, and do not the things which I say?" (Lk. 6:46).

This second main command is also found in Matthew 6, although different wording is used to communicate essentially the same message. Jesus has just given the negative command "Lay not up for yourselves treasures on earth." Now He tells us:

But lay up for yourselves treasures in heaven (Mt. 6:20).

In today's terminology, then, He is telling us to *accumulate wealth* in Heaven, to *invest* in Heaven, to *save for retirement* in Heaven. He is telling us, in essence, to make investments in

Heaven in much the same way that people of this world make investments on earth.

But how do we do this? What do we physically have to do to lay up treasure in Heaven? Luke 12:33 gives us the answer.

> Sell that ye have, and give alms; provide yourselves bags which wax not old, a *treasure in the heavens* that faileth not, where no thief approacheth, neither moth corrupteth.

So it's by *giving alms* that we can make a real investment in a real place called Heaven! And this investment is totally secure from all the problems (thieves, rust, recessions, inflation, and stock market corrections) associated with earthly investments! What's more, the rate of return is far better than that which any mutual fund manager has ever been able to consistently produce ("a hundredfold" according to Matthew 19:29).

The doctrine of nonaccumulation, therefore, means more than simply "don't accumulate." It also means, according to Luke 12:33, that we are to practice lavish generosity.

There are many people who don't accumulate earthly wealth, but at the same time do not really practice Biblical nonaccumulation. Perhaps because of either laziness or else excessive spending, they simply do not have any resources available to accumulate. Maybe they have even read Jesus' command not to lay up treasures on earth, and in response have cut back on their work, or have started to live in luxury, or have otherwise begun to squander those funds that they formerly had been putting into a savings account each month. In other words, they have stopped laying up treasures on earth, but have not started laying up treasures in Heaven. They simply are not laying up treasures *anywhere*.

But that is not Biblical nonaccumulation. This doctrine, rather, urges us to behave in many ways just like the people around us who are diligently saving for earthly retirement. We should work just as hard as they do (provided, of course, that our other responsibilities do not suffer). We should limit our personal spending just as they do. We should sell off poor investments, just as they do, to free up money to invest in something better. The primary difference is *where* we invest our money once we have it available to invest. Instead of putting it on earth, as they do, we make our investments in Heaven. And this is done through our giving.

Most Christians, even very wealthy ones, would state emphatically that they would be willing to sell their possessions and give away the proceeds if God asked them to do so. In no case would they walk sadly away from Christ as the rich young ruler did.

In other words, they are waiting for some sort of "triggering event," a "voice from the Lord," so to speak, telling them to sell and give. Although they don't really expect this triggering event to happen, if it ever should happen, they say, they would obey willingly without any delay.

Perhaps this describes your attitude. If so, then I commend you for your willingness to do anything for Jesus. I only urge you to stick with this commitment if this triggering event should ever come to pass.

I do have one question, however. What exactly would qualify as a triggering event? If a voice from the sky thundered out, "Sell and give," would that qualify? If you saw a hand writing "Sell and give" on the wall above your head, would that be enough to convince you that God is speaking?

What about Luke 12:33? Would reading that verse for the first time qualify as a triggering event?

Are we saying, then, that Jesus' command to us (Lk. 12:33) means exactly the same thing as the command He gave to the rich young ruler? Perhaps not, because there are differences with the language used in these two commands. On the other hand, perhaps so, because these differences are extremely minor.

As we compare the Luke 12:33 command with the command given in the story of the rich young ruler (Matthew 19, Mark 10, and Luke 18), here is what we find. The command given to the rich young ruler in Matthew's account is virtually identical to the command (given to us) in Luke 12:33. The commands given to the rich young ruler in Mark and Luke, however, contain the added word "all" that thou hast, or "whatsoever" thou hast.

Does this added word, then, prove a significant difference between that which God expects of us and that which he required of the rich young ruler? Was Jesus telling the rich young ruler to sell and give *everything* he owned, whereas He wants us only to sell and give *part* of what we own?

I'm not sure that I'm ready to answer this question once and for all. I will suggest an explanation, however, that seems to resolve this question and deal fairly with all the Scriptures involved.

It seems that Jesus, in both His command to us and His command to the rich young ruler, is telling us to distribute whatever possessions we do not currently need. In other words, sell and give those possessions that are clearly of an investment nature (as opposed to a "tool"). Sell and give those possessions that clearly qualify as "riches" (as opposed to basic needs such as food, clothing, shelter, and transportation). For someone as wealthy as the rich young ruler, this included virtually everything he owned. For someone who owns only two coats (Lk. 3:11), this would be only half of what he owns.

Whatever it is that Jesus means by His command in Luke 12:33, He does not intend for it to bring us into bondage, but rather to set us free. If we will but submit ourselves to this command, it becomes a doorway into some of the most wonderful opportunities we could possibly imagine. Once Jesus has set us free from the idea (produced by the society in which we live) that we need to be building up our earthly wealth, and has explained to us that giving to charity is actually an *investment* rather than an *expense*, we will begin to look at giving in an entirely new light. The opportunities in almsgiving are far more varied and exciting than earthly investing could ever be. Here are just a few examples of those opportunities:

- Christian Aid Ministries is able to get one Bible printed and delivered to a Christian in China for the small sum of $2. The revival going on right now in that country has produced far more Christians than there are Bibles. It has been estimated that for every Bible that goes into China, potentially 10 people will give their lives to Christ.

- Gospel for Asia can print and distribute eight New Testaments to India and surrounding countries for a donation of just $4.00. That's only $.50 each!

- Christian Aid Ministries has a program in which nearly $300 worth of material aid can be distributed for each dollar contributed. (This is because of the medicine and other products that manufacturers are willing to donate provided CAM pays for the shipping and handling costs.)

- Lighthouse Publishing prints a booklet, *Loaves and Fishes*, which is distributed for free in prisons around the country. The hunger for this sort of reading material is great, and there are enough requests that thousands more of these booklets could be passed out each year if funds would be available. One dollar is enough to print and ship one booklet to a spiritually hungry prisoner.

- Mount Zion Literature has recently had some wonderful opportunities open up in Cuba and Latin America for distributing gospel literature. (Remember that the impact of one book or tract is much greater in places such as these where God's Word is restricted than it is in America where we are saturated with Bibles and Christian books.) This ministry provides subsidies so that this literature can be taken to these countries and either given away or else sold at greatly reduced prices.

- Christian Aid Ministries' Seed Project is used to distribute vegetable seeds and gospel literature for free to needy individuals in poverty-stricken countries. A contribution of $25 to this program provides 15 families with enough seeds to produce a semi truck load of vegetables!

This is just a sampling of giving opportunities we have available, but they are enough to make the words of Jesus come alive when He said, "It is more blessed to give than to receive." Could there possibly be any earthly investment opportunity as exciting as those I have listed?

7

TESTING THE PILLARS

So far, we have looked at the two main commands of Christ on which the doctrine of nonaccumulation is built:

1. Lay not up for yourselves treasures on earth (Mt. 6:19).

2. Sell that ye have, and give alms (Lk. 12:33).

But how do these two commands stand up when we compare them with the rest of the New Testament? Does it still seem Biblical to say that they are to be taken literally? Or do other Scriptures "balance them out" enough to prove that they don't quite mean what they seem to be saying?

A number of other passages help to give us some answers to these questions.

What did John the Baptist teach?

John came preaching repentance, warning people to "flee from the wrath to come," and urging them to "bring forth fruits worthy of repentance." But, the people wondered, what are these fruits of repentance? Here is John's answer, in part.

> He that hath two coats, let him impart unto him that hath none; and he that hath meat, let him do likewise (Lk. 3:11).

I wonder how many of us, if asked to list the evidences of true repentance, would include this action in our list!

This verse also gives us some clues regarding the question of "to what extent" we should obey Luke 12:33. Does the command mean that we may not own anything at all? Are we somehow supposed to renounce our ownership of the very shirt on our back? "No," says John, "but rather give away that portion of your possessions that is in excess of what you need" (yes, that does require us to make a judgment call).

What did the church in Acts teach?

If a command as radical as Luke 12:33 were really meant to be taken literally, it seems logical that we would have some sort of record of this command being put into practice by the first Christians. Here are a couple of passages that might throw some light on what the early church believed about the command to "sell and give."

> And all that believed were together, and had all things common; and *sold their possessions* and goods, and *parted* them to all men, as every man had need (Acts 2:44–45).

> Neither was there any among them that lacked: for as many as were possessors of lands or houses *sold them*, and brought the prices of the things that were sold, and laid them down at the apostles' feet: and *distribution* was made to every man according as he had need (Acts 4:34–35).

"But," I can hear some responding, "This practice didn't continue long. This was a short-term situation that took place only during this transition period."

Although I've heard this claim numerous times, I don't really see how it could be proven with Scripture. But even if it could, that doesn't address the real question. The real question is whether the Luke 12:33 command is meant to be taken literally or not.

These Christians believed so, and were doing their best to put it into practice in one way or another. Do we have the freedom to do any less?

What other examples of obedience to Luke 12:33 do we have?

Zacchaeus (Lk. 19:1–10)

> Jesus said that "salvation" had come to Zacchaeus' house. What evidence had He seen that this was true? It was, in part, his obedience to Luke 12:33.

The poor widow (Lk. 21:1–3)

> Most financial counselors would say that this widow was extremely irresponsible for her obedience to Luke 12:33. Yet Jesus commended her for it.
>
> This account also gives us some important insight about how God measures the size of our gift. Whereas we humans tend to look at the dollar amount given, it appears that God looks instead at the amount we have left over after the gift.

The Macedonians (2 Cor. 8:1–5)

> Moreover, brethren, we do you to wit of the grace of God bestowed on the churches of Macedonia; How that in a great trial of affliction the abundance of their joy and their deep poverty abounded unto the riches of their liberality. For to their power, I bear record, yea, and beyond their power they were willing of themselves; Praying us with much intreaty that we would receive the gift, and take upon us the fellowship of the ministering to the saints. And this they did, not as we hoped, but first gave their own selves to the Lord, and unto us by the will of God.

What other commands did Christ give?

Take therefore no thought for the morrow: for the morrow shall take thought for the things of itself (Mt. 6:34).

Give to every man that asketh of thee; and of him that taketh away thy goods ask them not again (Lk. 6:30).

And if any man will sue thee at the law, and take away thy coat, let him have thy cloak also (Mt. 5:40).

But love ye your enemies, and do good, and lend, hoping for nothing again (Lk. 6:35).

But rather give alms of such things as ye have; and, behold, all things are clean unto you (Lk. 11:41).

Whosoever he be of you that forsaketh not all that he hath, he cannot be my disciple (Lk. 14:33).

Freely ye have received, freely give (Mt. 10:8).

What did Paul teach?

For ye know the grace of our Lord Jesus Christ, that, *though he was rich, yet for your sakes he became poor,* that ye through his poverty might be rich. . . . For if there be first a willing mind, it is accepted *according to that a man hath, and not according to that he hath not.* For I mean not that other men be eased, and ye burdened: But by an equality, that now at this time your abundance may be a supply for their want, that their abundance also may be a supply for your want: *that there may be equality: As it is written, He that had gathered much had nothing over; and he that had gathered little had no lack* (2 Cor. 8:9–15).

But this I say, He which soweth sparingly shall reap also sparingly; and he which soweth bountifully shall reap also bountifully. Every man according as he purposeth in his heart, so let him give; not grudgingly, or of necessity: for *God loveth a cheerful giver.* And God is able to make all grace abound toward you; that ye, always having all sufficiency in all things, may abound to every good work: As it is written, *He hath dispersed abroad; he hath given to the poor*: his righteousness remaineth for ever (2 Cor. 9:6–9).

Whiles by the experiment of this ministration they glorify God for your professed *subjection unto the gospel of Christ*, and for your liberal distribution unto them, and unto all men (2 Cor. 9:13).

These Christians knew that true subjection to the gospel of Christ included practicing the kind of generosity commanded in Luke 12:33.

As we have therefore opportunity, let us do good unto all men, especially unto them who are of the household of faith (Gal. 6:10).

Can we honestly say that we have done good "as we have opportunity" if we have money parked permanently in a savings account or retirement plan at the same time that there are needy people in the world?

But godliness with contentment is great gain. For we brought nothing into this world, and it is certain we can carry nothing out. And having food and raiment let us be therewith content. But they that will be rich fall into temptation and a snare, and into many foolish and hurtful lusts, which drown men in destruction and perdition. For the love of money is the root of all evil: which while some coveted after, they have *erred from the faith,* and pierced

themselves through with many sorrows. But thou, O man
of God, flee these things (1 Tim. 6:6–11).

The Christianity of Paul's day required men to "err from the
faith" if they wanted to covet after money. The Christianity that
we've developed allows men to covet after money and still
consider themselves to be "in the faith"!

Charge them that are rich in this world, that they be not
highminded, nor trust in uncertain riches, but in the living
God, who giveth us richly all things to enjoy; That they do
good, that they be rich in good works, *ready to distribute,*
willing to communicate (1 Tim. 6:17–18).

In other words, charge them to be willing to obey Luke 12:33.
But what is the purpose for their obedience to Luke 12:33?

Laying up in store for themselves a good foundation
against the time to come, *that they may lay hold on eternal life*
(1 Tim. 6:19).

What do the Scriptures say about those who are poor?

There is a widely held belief that because it's just as possible for
a poor person to be greedy for money as it is for a rich person,
there is no real benefit to being poor. What do the Scriptures
say about this?

He hath anointed me to preach the gospel to the poor (Lk.
4:18).

Blessed be ye poor: for yours is the kingdom of God (Lk.
6:20).

Hath not God chosen the poor of this world rich in faith, and heirs of the kingdom which he hath promised to them that love him? (Jas. 2:5).

What do the Scriptures say about those who are rich?

Another popular belief maintains that it's okay for a Christian to be rich, as long as he doesn't get too attached to his riches. Do the Scriptures bear this out?

He hath filled the hungry with good things; and the rich he hath sent empty away (Lk. 1:53).

But woe unto you that are rich! For ye have received your consolation (Lk. 6:24).

But Abraham said, Son, remember that thou in thy lifetime receivedst thy good things, and likewise Lazarus evil things: but now he is comforted, and thou art tormented (Lk. 16:25).

Did you ever ask yourself what exactly was the sin of the rich man in Luke 16, and what was the reason he ended up in the torments of Hell? Although we could speculate about many possible reasons, the one listed in the preceding verse is the only one mentioned in Scripture.

It is easier for a camel to go through the eye of a needle, than for a rich man to enter into the kingdom of God (Mt. 19:24).

If we really believed this verse, we would have to recognize what tremendous harm we are doing our children by trying to leave them financially wealthy.

Go to now, ye rich men, weep and howl for your miseries
that shall come upon you. Your riches are corrupted, and
your garments are *moth-eaten*. Your gold and silver is
cankered; and the *rust* of them shall be a witness against
you, and shall eat your flesh as it were fire. *Ye have heaped
treasure together for the last days.* . . . Ye have lived in
pleasure on the earth, and been wanton; ye have
nourished your hearts, as in a day of slaughter (Jas. 5:1–3,
5).

It's worth noting that the riches mentioned in this passage are
"heaped together" assets (as opposed to income simply passing
through a person's hands). Jesus warns in Matthew 6:19 that
this kind of "laid up" riches will become vulnerable to "moth"
and "rust," and that is exactly what has happened here. This
rust, in turn, will rise up against the owner as a witness that he
has violated the commandment of Christ.

They that will be rich fall into temptation and a snare . . .
but thou, O man of God, flee these things (1 Tim. 6:9, 11).

Because thou sayest, I am rich, and increased with goods,
and have need of nothing; and knowest not that thou art
wretched, and miserable, and poor, and blind, and naked
(Rev. 3:17).

8

A LESSON FROM HISTORY

T he year 1525 marked the beginning of one of the most powerful revivals in the history of the Christian church. Beginning with three men who baptized each other contrary to the teachings of the state church, this revival swept through Europe like a wildfire. Stressing a renewed focus on Christ as Lord of our lives, on unconditional love for all mankind, and on literal obedience to the Word of God, these Swiss Brethren (also labeled as Anabaptists) preached the gospel of Jesus everywhere they went.

"By the blood of the Lamb, and by the word of their testimony," these men relentlessly spread the Word of truth throughout a hungry society, and repentant sinners joined their ranks by the thousands. However, they also incurred the wrath of the governing authorities of the day, and horrible persecution broke out. Thousands upon thousands of these believers were slaughtered in the most gruesome ways imaginable. In response, the survivors began to flee from city to city and from country to country, always carrying with them this radical message of the kingdom of God.

This revival soon spread to the country of Holland, where another group of Anabaptists began to form called the Mennonites. They also preached the gospel faithfully and experienced the same rapid growth as multitudes one by one humbly bowed the knee and surrendered themselves to the lordship of Jesus Christ. But they also faced intense persecution. At one point, all criminals (including murderers) in the country were offered freedom, a pardon from the Emperor, and one hundred guilders if they could deliver the Anabaptist preacher Menno Simons into the hands of the torturers and executioners.

Eventually, however, the persecution ended, and these Dutch Mennonites began to gain acceptance as upstanding members of society. Their outstanding growth continued for a time, so that by the late 1600s there were approximately 160,000 of them living in Holland. This wonderful time of peace, together with a strong work ethic and a frugal lifestyle, led these Anabaptists into a time of great prosperity. Many of them were soon ranking among the wealthiest members of society and wielding great influence in the social and political realms. By all appearances, God was pouring out blessings on His church as never before. The years of hardship were over, and success, it seemed, had finally arrived.

But in the midst of this peace and prosperity something strange began to happen. Instead of the amazing growth these Anabaptists had experienced in their early years, their numbers started to decline drastically. Instead of pulling people in from the world around them and making them disciples of Jesus, it seemed that they had all they could do just to keep their own children in the faith. This trend continued until, within a period of about 100 years, their numbers had shrunk from 160,000 to fewer than 28,000.

What was it that went wrong? What caused the sudden powerlessness in this group of Christians called the Mennonites? In what way were the Dutch Mennonites of the 1600s different from the Swiss Brethren of the 1500s?

If you had asked a young Mennonite minister in the year 1680 to describe the differences between the beliefs of his church and the beliefs of the Swiss Brethren 150 years earlier, I can imagine that his answer would have gone something like this: "Well, *doctrinally* we believe everything pretty much the same as they did. *Practically*, however, we certainly do some things differently than they."

But would that have been true? Were the main differences only in practice? Or were there major doctrinal differences as well?

The answer to this question finally comes down to our definition of the word "doctrine." We humans have a tendency to simply change our vocabulary as our culture changes. When the practical outworking of a particular teaching becomes unpopular, we simply stop labeling it as a "doctrine." Thus, we can continue to glibly say that "our doctrine has not changed."

In truth, there were doctrinal differences between these two groups. The early Swiss Brethren had both taught and practiced the doctrine of nonaccumulation. The 17th-century Dutch Mennonites seemingly didn't teach or practice it. One writer, describing the change in their attitude toward the world, makes these statements:

> Originally the ideal was "in the world but not of the world"; later it was "free in and of the world." . . . For such freedom of activity, as was desired, material prosperity was necessary. [Horsch, p. 255]

On July 25, 1659, Thieleman J. van Braght wrote an introduction to his book, *Martyrs Mirror*. In this introduction he warned his people, the Dutch Mennonites, that the danger they were facing from prosperity and worldliness was far greater than the danger their fathers had faced from martyrdom.

Was van Braght correct? Was it true that a wrong view of earthly possessions was a leading cause of the spiritual decline? Or were the two totally unrelated to each other? Would faithful teaching of the doctrine of nonaccumulation have provided at least a small barrier against the tragedy that these people faced?

As Christians living in a country such as the United States of America, what lesson would God want us to learn from this account?

9

BEWARE OF COVETOUSNESS

Jesus commands in Luke 12:15, "Beware of covetousness." What does He mean?

"Covetousness" has traditionally been interpreted to mean "a desire for something that belongs to somebody else." Although that certainly is a dangerous desire, it is not exactly what Jesus is warning us to beware. Rather, the "covetousness" that Jesus is warning us against has simply the meaning of "a desire for more."

If this is true, then it is a serious warning to us who live in a country such as America. Whereas the former definition of covetousness says, "Give me what is yours," the latter says, "You can keep what is yours, and I'll go get one of my own." This latter form of covetousness can be gratified without breaking any laws or harming another person. It is exactly what we are encouraged to do in our capitalistic society.

The true test for covetousness, therefore, is not the question, "Do I have a desire for something that belongs to someone else?" nor even "Do I have a desire to be rich?" (Most Christians would answer "no" to both of these questions.) The real question we should ask ourselves, rather, is "Do I have a desire to be richer than I am right now?"

Or, to put it another way, "Do I desire to own more possessions a year from now than what I do today?"

The opposite of covetousness is *contentment*. Hebrews 13:5 tells us to be content "with such things as ye have." 1 Timothy 6:8 tells us to be content "with food and raiment." Yet how many of us *claim* to be content with what we have, while at the same time we are struggling mightily to increase our level of wealth?

The twin commands of Jesus to "lay not up" (Matthew 6:19) and to "sell and give" (Luke 12:33) strike right at the heart of this deceptive sin of covetousness. Whereas the first command forbids us to try to *increase* our possessions, the second one tells us we should actually make plans to own *less* in the future than what we do now.

And what if we choose to ignore these warnings? Can we still consider ourselves to be part of the body of Christ? Here is what the Scriptures say:

> But fornication, and all uncleanness, *or covetousness,* let it not once be named among you (Eph. 5:3).

> No whoremonger, nor unclean person, *nor covetous man,* who is an idolater, hath any inheritance in the kingdom of Christ and of God (Eph. 5:5).

> Mortify therefore your members which are upon the earth; fornication, uncleanness, inordinate affection, evil concupiscence, *and covetousness,* which is idolatry: for which things sake the wrath of God cometh on the children of disobedience (Col. 3:5–6).

> I have written unto you not to keep company, if any man that is called a brother be a fornicator, *or covetous,* or an idolater . . . with such an one no not to eat (1 Cor. 5:11).

> They that will be rich fall into a temptation and a snare, and into many foolish and hurtful lusts, which drown men in destruction and perdition. For the love of money is the root of all evil, which while some *coveted* after, they have erred from the faith, and pierced themselves through with many sorrows. But thou, O man of God, flee these things (1 Tim. 6:9–11).

10

THE "WHY" OF
NONACCUMULATION

When we are given a command by God, we shouldn't have to ask the reasons why. The simple fact that God has commanded it ought to be enough for us. However, God in his mercy has given us a number of reasons why we should obey the doctrine of nonaccumulation.

Because it keeps our heart on things above

> For where your treasure is, there will your heart be also (Mt. 6:21).

According to Jesus, our heart will follow our possessions. If we lay them up on earth, our heart will be on earth. If we lay them up in Heaven, our heart will be in Heaven.

Because mammon (wealth) is an alternate god

Jesus says, "Ye cannot serve God and mammon," and for a very good reason. Wealth seeks to offer us many of the things God Himself desires to give us. Wealth offers us security, influence, health, happiness, love, and power. However, the forms of these things offered by wealth are deceptive counterfeits of the genuine forms offered by God alone. To accept the forgeries offered by wealth will lead ultimately to disappointment and ruin. To reject wealth's counterfeits and choose the "real thing" offered by God will lead to fulfillment and eternal life.

Because it allows us really to love others as we love ourselves

> But whoso hath this world's good, and seeth his brother have need, and shutteth up his bowels of compassion from him, how dwelleth the love of God in him? (1 Jn. 3:17)

Even without any other supporting Scriptures, this verse alone ought to be enough to convince us that the doctrine of nonaccumulation is true.

Because it follows the example of Jesus (1 Jn. 2:6, Jn. 12:26)

We could ask some important questions. Did Jesus accumulate wealth on this earth? Did He leave behind a store of wealth for his disciples to split among themselves? Or did He say goodbye to this world carrying "nothing but the clothes on His back"? If we are to follow His example, what does this tell us?

Because it sets us free to truly seek first the kingdom of God (Mt. 6:33)

Once we have been set free from the perception that we need to be saving up money for retirement or a possible medical bill, we can put all our extra resources—time, talents, and possessions—into building God's kingdom.

Because it builds faith in God

To accumulate wealth as a safety net against hard times almost forces us to trust in that wealth. On the other hand, to refuse to accumulate is an active step of faith that says, "Lord, I will obey your commands even if it looks extremely risky to do so. I'm trusting you to do what you've promised to do in response to this obedience." In taking this step, we actually put ourselves in a far safer position than if we refuse to take this step.

Because it draws us closer to each other

Something special happens in a brotherhood where everyone is working hard, investing all their excess funds into the work of our King, and laying nothing aside (on this earth) for the future. We have to recognize that it likely will be this same group of brothers that God will use to supply our physical needs at some point in the future.

Because it removes a major source of jealousy among brothers in the Church

Financial dealings between brothers always pose potential for misunderstandings and hard feelings. Suppose, for instance, that a Christian businessman hires a Christian employee and pays him less than what the employee thinks he ought to be paid. Or suppose that one Christian brother charges another brother what seems like too much for some work he has performed. (Such situations ought to be very rare if we strive to practice the Biblical principles of mutual love and brotherhood equality.)

In the world's economy, either of these situations would likely be a cause for bitterness to arise. If, however, both brothers involved in the transaction believe and practice Biblical nonaccumulation, these issues become much less significant. Each of us knows that the other brother, if he makes an excessive profit at my expense, won't keep this profit for himself. Rather, he will put it very soon into the work of building God's kingdom, which is the same place it would have gone if the money had passed through my hands first.

Because God has promised to supply our needs

But my God shall supply all your need according to his riches in glory by Christ Jesus (Phil. 4:19).

The fact that God will supply our needs is one of the primary reasons for nonaccumulation given by Jesus in Matthew 6:25-34, immediately after the command to "lay not up."

Because to accumulate on earth is a waste of resources that could be used to build Christ's kingdom

Some will say, "I earn enough money that I can give generously and still save for retirement." (In other words, I can lay up treasures on earth *and* in Heaven.) In a sense, that is true. One *person* can both give to charity and store up on earth at the same time. But he cannot do it *with the same money*. The money he gives, he cannot store up on earth. That which he stores up on earth he cannot give until he ceases to store it up.

Because to accumulate on earth is simply a poor investment

Where moth and rust doth corrupt, and where thieves break through and steal (Mt. 6:19).

Treasures on earth simply don't last very long, no matter how well you try to protect them. I have heard people say, "Land is a good investment. It always increases in value in the long term." Or "The long-term trend of the stock market is that it will go up." But no matter how many statistics you can quote or charts you can produce to support these statements, they are both absolutely false. According to God's Word, the truly long-term trend of both land and stocks is down!

The earth . . . shall be burned up . . . all these things shall be dissolved (2 Pet. 3:10–11).

Because to accumulate on earth robs the owner of the right to enjoy the fruits of his own labor

God asked the rich farmer in Luke 12, "Then whose shall these things be?" This man had worked very hard and had produced a lot of resources. But because he had laid them up on earth, they were snatched from his hands at the point of death, and he would never have the privilege of enjoying those fruits. If he had laid them up in Heaven, however, he could have enjoyed them through all eternity.

11

BUT WHAT ABOUT ANANIAS AND SAPPHIRA?

One passage of Scripture often used in an attempt to refute the doctrine of nonaccumulation is the story of Ananias and Sapphira in Acts 5:1–11. After they had sold some land and brought part of the money to the apostles, this couple lied and said they had brought all of the money. Peter's response in verse 4 indicates that they should not have lied because, after all, *it was their choice* whether they sold the land or not. And once it was sold, *it was their choice* as to how much of the money they would bring to the apostles.

Because of this statement by Peter, some say the doctrine of nonaccumulation must be false. Luke 12:33 must not be binding on us. The command to sell and give must have been meant for some era other than the one in which we are now living.

However, Peter didn't say that the Luke 12:33 command had somehow been nullified. On the contrary, he was still doing his best to follow Christ's injunction in Matthew 28:20, where He says his followers are to "teach them to observe all things that I've commanded you" (including the command in Luke 12:33).

So what was it that Peter was saying by this statement? He was merely affirming the voluntary nature of the gospel of Christ. Every part of the gospel, including Luke 12:33, is to be a product of the hearer's free will. Repenting is to be done voluntarily. Confession is to be done voluntarily. Receiving baptism is an exercise of the free will. And obedience to Christ's commands is to come from a heart of joyful, willing submission to our King.

The apostles were not forcing anyone to sell and give. Because Luke 12:33 is part of Christ's gospel, we can be sure that they promoted it, preached it, and practiced it. But it was carried out by the willing hearts of the new believers, not by the apostles imposing their wills on others through force or coercion. And the people's response (according to Acts 2:41–47 and Acts 4:31–37) was loving, heartfelt obedience to Christ.

Not only was the question of *whether* to obey Luke 12:33 left in the hands of the people, but also the question of *to what extent* they should put it into practice. Some of the people sold most of their possessions immediately. Others no doubt began selling off property as the opportunities arose in the real estate market or as needs arose in the church. But no one seemed to believe that Luke 12:33 could simply be ignored if one wanted to call oneself a believer in Jesus.

This point is reinforced by the fact that even Ananias and Sapphira, with their covetous, hypocritical hearts, knew that obedience to Luke 12:33 was a definite part of being a follower of Christ. Therefore, they did their best to at least *appear* to be obedient to this command, even if they had to lie to do it.

12

BUT WHAT ABOUT THE
PARABLE OF THE TALENTS?

There probably is no passage used more frequently to justify the accumulation of earthly wealth than the Parable of the Talents.

In this parable, found in Matthew 25 and Luke 19, Jesus tells of a master who was going to be taking an extended trip into a foreign country. Before he left, he divided up his money among his servants and told them to invest it wisely until he returned. At his return some time later, these servants were rewarded or punished on the basis of how well they had done in the world of investing.

The logic used is simple. Because a key part of Jesus' parable is about *earthly investing*, and because the rewards go to those who have done well at earthly investing, Jesus must therefore approve of earthly investing.

This logic has several problems. First, Jesus frequently uses *earthly* activities in his parables to teach a *spiritual* lesson. In Luke 14:31, for instance, He uses the example of going to war to teach a lesson about commitment. Does that mean he approves of us going to war? Or what about building a tower, sowing seed, or putting on a banquet? Does the fact that Jesus uses these activities in His parables prove that He is advocating their practice? Hardly. It is far more reasonable to believe that the earthly activity given in the parable is a *type* of some corresponding spiritual activity.

Second, does it seem reasonable that Jesus would *forbid* earthly investing in Matthew 6:19, give warning after warning about earthly riches throughout His teaching, and then turn around and *promote* earthly investing in one of His parables?

Many theories have been suggested about what Jesus actually is trying to teach in the parable of the talents. Many teach, as mentioned earlier, that Jesus is giving us a lesson on how to handle earthly wealth. Others say that Jesus is teaching us what to do with our talents or abilities. Still others say that the point of the parable is that we are to be good stewards of our time, or of our children, or of the friends that we have been given.

I remember a group discussion about this parable one Sunday morning. Although no one seemed very sure about its meaning, many ideas were suggested, including some of the aforementioned ideas.

Then I raised my hand and gave my suggestion about the meaning of this parable. Jesus is teaching us that we should be good stewards, I reasoned, but He is not singling out one particular thing such as our money, our time, or our abilities. Rather, He is teaching us to be good stewards of *everything* we own, including our money, our time, and our abilities. I was pleased with my clever answer, and everyone present also seemed to accept it as satisfactory.

Years later, I began to recognize that although my statement was true (we should be good stewards of all we own), it isn't at all the point Jesus is making with this parable. This explanation simply doesn't fit the features of this parable as Jesus tells it.

The key to understanding any parable is to identify the symbols used in the actual story, and then to ask the question, "What do these symbols typify?"

The primary symbols in this parable are the master, the servants, and the money. I think we all can agree that the master represents Jesus Himself. The servants, then, represent His followers, or us as Christians. (Luke 19:13–14 makes a clear distinction between the *servants* and the rest of the *citizens* of that country.)

But what exactly is it that the *money* represents? If we can answer this question correctly, then we are well on our way to understanding the entire parable. The following are some attributes of the money in Jesus' parable, so these same attributes ought to be found in whatever it is that the money represents:

- Whatever it is that the money typifies, we know it is something Jesus gave to His followers, and to His followers alone. (The *citizens* did not receive any of it.)

- Whatever it is that the money typifies, it is something that must be *increased* during the time that it is in our possession. (Keeping it in its original condition was not at all satisfactory.)

- Whatever it is that the money typifies, it is something that must be *returned* to Jesus when he comes back for us.

With these characteristics as the criteria, let's ask again: What *does* the money typify? Do any of the traditional answers fit, such as our abilities, our time, or our possessions? Not really. First of all, time, abilities, and possessions are given to *all* men, not just to Christians.

What about the idea of *increasing* these things? Will we be rewarded on the basis of how much we have increased our earthly wealth? I don't think so. What about our time? If God gives us 70 years to live, are we supposed to somehow increase that to 80 years? Even if we could, we would still have *less* time left at the end of our lives than at the beginning, not more. How about our abilities? These can be increased, it is true, but generally those abilities we have gained during our lifetime start to fade away quickly in the last years of life.

When we examine the idea of returning these things to Jesus, the traditional answers don't fit very well either. None of us will have any time, talents, or money that we can hand over to Christ on judgment day. All these things will be utterly worthless at that point!

The truth about the meaning of this parable became suddenly obvious to me one day when I read a book that explained what the early Christians believed about its meaning. They did not believe that Jesus is teaching us how to use money, possessions, time, talents, or relationships. Rather, the money in this parable symbolizes nothing more or less than the kingdom of God (or the *gospel* of the kingdom, or the *mysteries* of the kingdom).

When I heard this explanation, everything suddenly snapped into place regarding the meaning of this parable. It began to make sense to me in a way that it never had before. The kingdom of God was something that Jesus gave to his disciples, but not to the other residents of this planet. It is something that we are expected to *increase* during the time that it is in our power to do so. And it is something that we must ultimately *return* to our Lord Jesus to do with as He pleases.

Further confirmation that this interpretation is the correct one can be found in the explanatory verse of the parable itself.

> For I say unto you, that unto every one which hath shall be given: and from him that hath not, even that he hath shall be taken away from him (Lk. 19:26).

This verse by itself doesn't provide much clarification until we look at another passage that is a parallel passage to this one.

> For whosoever hath, to him shall be given, and he shall have more abundance: but whosoever hath not, from him shall be taken away even that he hath (Mt. 13:12).

So what is this verse talking about? What is this commodity that is being either *given* or else *taken away*? Let's back up one verse to see.

> Because it is given unto you to know the *mysteries of the kingdom of Heaven*, but to them it is not given (Mt. 13:11).

It is obvious that the parable of the talents is given to provide us with a very important lesson on the subject of stewardship. But does the Scripture give any more clues that would shed some light on what kind of stewardship it is talking about, what exactly it is that we are to be stewards of? Here is one more passage that seems worth mentioning.

> Moreover it is required in stewards, that a man be found faithful (1 Cor. 4:2).

Is this referring primarily to our stewardship of possessions? Or of our time? Or perhaps of our abilities? Again let's back up a verse and see.

> Let a man so account of us, as of the ministers of Christ, and *stewards of the mysteries of God.* (1 Cor. 4:1).

13

THE PARABLE OF
THE UNJUST STEWARD

The Parable of the Talents obviously is not a lesson on financial stewardship. However, this doesn't mean that Jesus does not teach on this subject. Nor does it mean that He doesn't give any parables that deal with the subject of economics. On the contrary, Jesus gives a tremendous amount of instruction on how we are to use earthly wealth. He wants us to be good stewards of our earthly possession, and one of the best lessons He gives on financial stewardship is in the Parable of the Unjust Steward, found in Luke 16:1-15. (Jesus says very clearly in verses 9, 11, and 13 that this entire lesson is about how we are to use *mammon*, or earthly wealth.)

This story is about a steward employed by a rich man to manage his possessions. These possessions did not belong to the steward. They were only entrusted to him for a time. During that time, however, he apparently had been given the privilege to do with his master's possessions almost anything he wished. Upon finding out that he would soon be losing his job, this steward wisely went out and gave away his master's possessions, thus making friends who could take care of him after his stewardship position had ended.

Many people read this parable and shake their heads in confusion. "This man was *dishonest*," they say. "He actually *stole* from his employer!"

But was it really stealing? Not necessarily. What this man did was stealing only if he was doing something he had not been given the authority to do. Isn't it entirely possible that as a steward of his master's possessions he had been given the right to do almost anything he pleased, including giving the stuff away? (The response of the master in verse 8 certainly indicates that this steward had not exceeded the authority he had been given.)

Furthermore, this story is a type of our stewardship position under God, and it is certainly true that we have been given this level of authority over the possessions He has entrusted to us. We have been given the power to keep them, sell them, repair them, destroy them, or give them away, totally at our discretion! So is it stealing when we give away our possessions? Of course not, because the actual owner has given us the authority to do so.

This parable, instead of condoning stealing, is a beautiful type of the stewardship position we occupy as humans.

- Like the steward in this parable, we have been entrusted with property that actually belongs to Someone else—God.

- Like this steward, we will someday give account for what we have done with this property.

- Like this steward, we have been given notice that the time we have in our stewardship position is rapidly coming to a close.

- Like this steward, the decisions we make today about what to do with our Lord's money will have a direct impact on our well-being after our stewardship time has ended.

- Like this steward, the key to our future security lies in *giving these things away,* not in keeping them for ourselves. To try to keep them is to lose them forever. To give them away is to keep them eternally.

14

MORE OBJECTIONS TO NONACCUMULATION

Despite the abundance of support in Scripture for the doctrine of nonaccumulation, there will always be people who use Scriptures and logic in attempts to disprove it. Here are a few of the more common objections some have used.

Paul wrote about the *rich* in 1 Timothy 6:17–19 as though they were part of the church. Doesn't this prove that Luke 12:33 doesn't apply to us?

Luke 12:33 is a command for us to "distribute." Let's read the passage in Timothy to see if it supports or refutes this command. Here is what it says, in part:

> Charge them that are rich in this world . . . that they be . . . ready to distribute . . . that they may lay hold on eternal life.

Nowhere do we read in this passage that the commands in Matthew 6:19 or Luke 12:33 have been rescinded. Rather, Paul seems to be saying that these commands apply to the rich just as they do to everyone else.

The term "rich" can apply either to those who are rich in *income* (who earn $1 million a year) or to those who are rich in *assets* (who have $1 million in a bank account). The Bible doesn't condemn those who are rich in income as long as they obey Matthew 6:19 (by not laying up treasures on earth) and Luke 12:33 (by distributing to those in need at every opportunity).

Nor does the Bible condemn someone who is rich in assets, provided he did not acquire those assets through disobedience to Matthew 6:19. Perhaps he received the money through inheritance. Or perhaps he already had the money at the time he became a Christian. Either way, the requirements are the same for him as they are for everyone else: stop laying up treasures on earth (Mt. 6:19) and start distributing that which he currently has (Lk. 12:33). In doing so, he will follow the example of our Lord Jesus, who "though he was rich, yet for your sakes he became poor, that ye through his poverty might become rich."

Proverbs 6:6 tells us to follow the example of the ant in laying up treasures for the future. Doesn't this disprove the doctrine of nonaccumulation?

The doctrine of nonaccumulation does not teach that we shouldn't lay up for the future. On the contrary, Matthew 6:20 actually *commands* us to lay up for the future. The prohibition, rather, is that we are not to lay up on earth, but rather in Heaven.

The key issue here is the question of where we are going to spend our future. Because an ant will spend her future in an anthill somewhere, she ought to be laying up treasures in an anthill. Because our future will be spent in Heaven, we ought to be laying up our treasures in Heaven.

Some people, who because of either laziness or poor management, are not able to lay up treasures anywhere, either on earth or in Heaven. These people need to read Proverbs 6:6, receive the warning it gives, and repent of their slothfulness. Then they ought to get up, get busy, earn money, and start laying up treasures. The only stipulation is that their laying up must be in Heaven (through giving) and not on earth (through hoarding).

1 Timothy 5:8 tells us we need to provide for our own. Doesn't that include laying up treasures on earth?

This passage in 1 Timothy 5 makes sense only in the context of a church in which nonaccumulation is being practiced. The key is to recognize that this verse is talking about providing for the older generation, not the younger one.

The dilemma here is that of some widows whose husbands had not accumulated wealth on earth (in obedience to Matthew 6:19). Consequently, these widows had nothing with which to support themselves in their old age. The solution Paul gives is that family members should take first responsibility to support these widows, and, where that failed, the church should take over.

Paul was showing clearly how a Biblical church ought to provide for the needs of its elderly members. In churches where this is practiced consistently, the temptation to violate Matthew 6:19 and Luke 12:33 is greatly reduced. The younger members can feel free to devote all their assets to the work of the Lord (including the care of the elderly), knowing that the rest of the church will be perfectly willing to provide for *them* if they should ever lose their ability to provide for themselves.

2 Corinthians 12:14 says the parents ought to lay up for the children (and not the other way around). Doesn't this disprove the doctrine of nonaccumulation?

Using this verse, in part, as support for their actions, many parents spend a good portion of their lives storing up wealth so they can leave a sizeable financial inheritance to their children. Countless families have consequentially been plagued by bitter feuding, intoxicating materialism, and spiritual ruin as a result of the sudden wealth thrust upon them. Countless other parent–child relationships have been strained while the parents were yet alive because of the children's secret desire for the parents to die so that they could get their hands on the money. Still other situations have resulted in virtually nothing being passed on to the heirs because of high court costs and attorney fees.

Although it seems more likely that Paul is referring here to providing for the current needs of our children, it is entirely possible that he is referring to the customary practice of leaving a financial inheritance. Either way, he clearly is using it for *illustrative* purposes, not for *instructional* purposes (very similar to the way he uses the illustration of a soldier in 2 Timothy 2:4 and of an athlete in 2 Timothy 2:5).

Paul is simply trying to assure the Corinthians that he is not after the material things that they could provide for him, although he would have had the full right to receive such a provision. He therefore indicates, through this illustration, that he is willing to assume the role of a parent with very young children. Young children, you see, never feel any twinge of conscience for not providing for the needs of their parents.

No matter what the practice is to which Paul refers, it is obvious from the context that the issue at hand is the provision of his current needs, not the storing up of reserves for the future. The question of whether Paul approved of stockpiling financial resources or not can be quickly resolved simply by going back a few chapters and reading 2 Corinthians 8 and 9.

Let us assume for just a moment, however, that 1 Corinthians 12:14 is a command to leave an inheritance to our children. This would make it a parallel verse to Proverbs 13:22, which says that "a good man leaveth an inheritance to his children's children." In this proverb we can see the clear difference between the diligent dad, who faithfully stores up assets to pass on to his descendants, and the deadbeat dad, who squanders all his earnings on himself during his own lifetime.

If you are a diligent father in that you desire to leave your children with a sizeable inheritance, you probably have already recognized that to do so will require a lot of hard work and sacrifice on your part. It will require faithfulness about putting a portion of your earnings into safekeeping for them each month. Here, then, is the all-important question: where are you going to store this wealth that you will be laying aside for your family? In a bank account? In the stock market? In the family farm? In rental property? In gold coins buried in your back yard? But all these things are earthly investments, which Jesus said are likely to be spoiled by moth, rust, and thieves! Why would you want to take such a gamble? Why would you play the fool with your children's inheritance? Why not rather, in response to Jesus' counsel, help your children store up this wealth for themselves in Heaven, "where no thief approacheth, neither moth corrupteth"?

Many Godly men in the Old Testament such as Abraham and Job were very rich. Doesn't this disprove the doctrine of nonaccumulation?

One foundational principle of the doctrine of nonaccumulation is that God's requirements for His people are different in the New Testament from what they were in the Old Testament. Christ introduced us to a brand new covenant with its own set of commands, many of which had not been commanded to God's people under the old covenant.

Jesus says repeatedly in His Sermon on the Mount "It hath been said . . . but I say unto you." These statements highlight a number of differences between the Law given by Moses and the laws of the kingdom of God. Under the old covenant, God at times commanded his people to destroy their enemies. Under the new covenant, we are commanded to love them. Under the old covenant, divorce and remarriage was permitted in some cases. Under the new covenant, it is strictly forbidden. Under the old covenant, laying up treasures on earth was permitted or even commanded. Under the new covenant, Jesus forbids us to accumulate wealth on earth.

Wasn't Joseph of Arimathaea a rich man in the New Testament?

Scripture's first mention of Joseph of Arimathaea is at the time of the crucifixion when he came and asked Pilate for Christ's body and then buried it in his own tomb. Matthew 27:57 calls him a "disciple," and Luke 23:51 says that he "waited for the kingdom of God."

So how did Joseph of Arimathaea respond to Luke 12:33 once this kingdom (for which he was waiting) had come to fruition? Acts 2:44–45 says that "all" the believers took part in obeying this command, and that must have included Joseph of Arimathaea. No reliable Bible version in circulation today reads that "all the believers except Joseph of Arimathaea" obeyed this command.

The command to "sell and give" applied only to the rich young ruler, didn't it?

That this argument is even used at all simply reveals a widespread ignorance of the fact that Luke 12:33 is in the Bible. When you take Luke 12:33 out of the Bible, then this argument seems as though it may have some merit. When you put Luke 12:33 back in the Bible, however, this argument is turned totally upside down.

First, remember that the Luke 12:33 command was given to Christ's *disciples* (and therefore to us). The rich young ruler isn't mentioned at all in Luke 12.

Second, Luke 12:33 was given *before* the story of the rich ruler, not after it. At the time Jesus gave the Luke 12:33 command, there may have been some doubt in the disciples' minds about whether this command was really meant to be taken literally. After they witnessed the encounter with the rich ruler six chapters later, however, there was no longer any doubt. This command was meant to be taken literally, they now realized, even by those who were rich.

In the story of Mary anointing Jesus with costly ointment, Jesus told Judas that we will have the poor with us always. (Mk. 14:3-9) By saying this, wasn't He de-emphasizing the importance of giving to the poor?

Throughout His earthly ministry Jesus preached about the importance of helping the poor. This is especially true in Matthew 25:31-46 where Jesus indicates that our eternal destiny will be determined to a large degree by how we have responded to the physical needs of our fellow man. He says in this passage that to give to the poor is to give to Him and to fail to give to the poor is to fail to give to Him.

After Mary had anointed Jesus with this costly ointment, Judas, in a show of loyalty to the teachings of Jesus, said that this ointment instead ought to have been sold and the money given to the poor (just as Jesus had commanded in Luke 12:33). Jesus, however, rebuked Judas and responded that "The poor always ye have with you; but me ye have not always." (Jn. 12:8)

Jesus' response to Judas was not a contradiction of the things he had been preaching the last three years. Rather, it was further confirmation of the truth that giving to the poor is the equivalent of giving to Christ Himself. Mary should not have been criticized for choosing to give to Christ directly instead of giving to the poor. After all, a desire to give to Christ was supposed to be the motivation for giving to the poor in the first place. Either of these two actions would have been giving to Jesus; either action would have been motivated by a love for Jesus.

If we have the kind of love for Christ that Mary did, we also will seek, as she did, to give generously to Him in one way or another. Because we do not have the option of giving to Christ in the flesh as Mary did, we must therefore choose the other way to give to our Lord: by giving to the poor. And there never will be a lack of opportunity to do so because, says Jesus, "The poor always ye have with you."

15

HAS ANYONE ELSE TAUGHT THIS DOCTRINE?

The doctrine of nonaccumulation has for so long been divorced from American Christianity that the renewed teaching of it sounds to many of us like pure heresy. But this was not always the case. This doctrine (whether it was called a "doctrine" or not) has been an important part of the teaching of many godly Christians in history. It has typically come to the forefront during times of revival, only to be lost during periods of apostasy.

The following groups of Christians, to some degree, taught and practiced this doctrine.

The Early Christians

The following quotes taken from *A Dictionary of Early Christian Beliefs* show how the early Christians viewed earthly wealth:

> These are the ones who have faith indeed, but they also have the riches of this world. As a result, when tribulation comes, they deny the Lord on account of their riches and business. . . . So also those who are rich in this world cannot be useful to the Lord unless their riches are cut down. [Hermas, p. 541]

> The good man, being temperate and just, treasures up his wealth in heaven. He who has sold his worldly goods and given them to the poor, finds the imperishable treasure "where there is neither moth nor robber.". . . It is not

jewels, gold, clothing, or beauty of person that are of high value, but virtue. [Clement of Alexandria, p. 541]

How can they follow Christ, who are held back by the chain of their wealth? . . . They think that they possess, but they are possessed instead. They are the bondslaves of their money, not the lords of their money. They are slaves of their profit. [Cyprian, p. 543]

He who desires to obtain justice, God, perpetual life, everlasting light, and all those things that God promises to man—he will scorn those riches, honors, commands, and kingdoms themselves. [Lactantius, p. 543]

A blind love of one's own property has deceived many. How could they be prepared for fleeing (in persecution) . . . when their wealth fettered them like a chain? . . . For that reason, the Lord, . . . forewarning for the future time, said, "If you will be perfect, go sell all that you have and give to the poor." If rich men did this, they would not perish because of their riches. . . . Heart, mind, and feeling would be in heaven, if the treasure were in heaven. [Cyprian, p. 441]

The Waldensians

The following is taken from *The Kingdom That Turned The World Upside Down.*

The Waldensians held to no complicated theological beliefs. Their belief system was basically the gospel of the kingdom. Knowing thoroughly the teachings of Jesus, they taught that we humans are capable of making choices. And we are responsible for the choices we make. We each must make the decision to live by the teachings Christ— and then be faithful to that decision. "No one can be a true

Christian," they said, "if he has not truly surrendered his life to the Lordship of Christ." They accurately saw that Jesus' teachings were revolutionary and that they were intended to be lived literally. *So they taught against the accumulation of wealth.* They also taught against using the sword for either self-defense or war. [Bercot, pp. 227, 228]

The Anabaptists

The following is an early Swiss Brethren "Congregational Order," which was attached to the Schleitheim Brotherly Union of 1527:

> Of all the brothers and sisters of this congregation none shall have anything of his own, but rather, as the Christians in the time of the apostles held all in common, and especially stored up a common fund, from which aid can be given to the poor, according as each will have need, and as in the apostles' time permit no brother to have need. [Yoder, pp. 44, 45]

Here is a quote from Leonhard Schiemer's "Letter to the Church of God at Rattenburg" written in the year 1527:

> How the heathen or nominal Christian pray. . . .They pray, "Give us today our daily bread." But as soon as God gives it to them it is no longer ours, but mine. And today is not enough but they worry about the next day against God's command when he commanded not to be concerned about the next day. They, however, are worried not only about the next day but about the whole year, and not only about one year but about ten, twenty, or thirty years. They are anxious not only for themselves, but for their children, not only as youth, but as adults.... [Snyder, pp. 77, 78]

Menno Simons, in his "Humble and Christian Defense" wrote this:

> It is not customary that an intelligent person clothes and cares for one part of his body and leaves the rest destitute and naked. Oh, no. The intelligent person is solicitous for all his members. Thus it should be with those who are the Lord's church and body. All those who are born of God, who are gifted with the Spirit of the Lord, and who, according to the Scriptures, are called into one body of love in Christ Jesus, are prepared by such love to serve their neighbors, not only with money and goods, but also after the example of their Lord and Head, Jesus Christ, in an evangelical manner, with life and blood. They show mercy and love, as much as they can; suffer no beggars amongst them; take to heart the need of the saints; receive the miserable; take the stranger into their houses; console the afflicted; assist the needy; clothe the naked; feed the hungry; do not turn their face from the poor, and do not despise their own flesh. [Simons, II:309]

Anna of Rotterdam, who was put to death for her faith in the year 1539, wrote a letter to her son Isaiah before she died. In this letter she gave him this counsel:

> Honor the Lord in the works of your hands, and let the light of the Gospel shine through you. Love your neighbor. Deal with an open, warm heart thy bread to the hungry, clothe the naked, and suffer not to have anything twofold; for there are always some who lack. Whatever the Lord grants you from the sweat of your face above what you need, communicate to those of whom you know that they love the Lord; and suffer nothing to remain in your possession until the morrow, and the Lord shall bless the work of your hands, and give you his blessing for an

inheritance. O my son, let your life be conformed to the Gospel. [*Martyrs Mirror*, pp. 453, 454]

John Wesley

From *The Language of the Deathbed*:

John Wesley detested the heartlessness of hoarding. One of the sharpest rebukes he ever administered, was in a sermon he preached in Dublin, in 1779, when he was an old man almost ready to leave this world. How the fire must have flashed from the lustrous eye as he proceeded to arraign his hearers after this fashion.

"O, that God would enable me once more, before I go hence and am not seen, to lift my voice like a trumpet to those who gain and save all they can, but do not give all they can! Ye are the men, some of the chief men, who continually grieve the Holy Spirit of God, and in a great measure stop the gracious influence from descending on our assemblies.

"Many of your brethren, beloved of God, have no food to eat; they have no raiment to put on; and not a place where to lay their head. And why are they thus distressed? Because you impiously, unjustly, and cruelly detain from them what your Master and theirs lodges in your hands on purpose to supply their wants! See that poor member of Christ, pinched with hunger, shivering with cold, half naked! Meantime you have plenty of this world's goods—food, drink, and apparel. In the name of God, what are you doing? Do you neither fear God, nor regard man? Why do you not deal your bread to the hungry, and cover the naked with a garment? Have you laid out in your own costly apparel what would have answered both these intentions, or covered you both? Did God command you to do so? Did he entrust you with these goods for this end? And does He now say, "Servant of God, well done?" You well know He does not. This idle expense has no approbation, either from God, or from your own conscience. But you say you can't afford it! O be ashamed to take such miserable nonsense into your mouth! Never more utter such a stupid cant; palpable absurdity! Can any steward afford to be an arrant knave to waste his Lord's goods? Can any servant afford to lay out his Master's money any otherwise than his Master appoints him? So far from it, that whoever does this ought to be excluded from a Christian society." [Stutzman, pp. 85, 86]

As Jonathan Huddleston observed:

Wesley used his own life as an example: "I gain all I can" in profitable labor; "I save all I can" by frugal living; and "by giving all I can, I am effectually secured from 'laying up treasures on earth.'" These were no idle boasts: As Wesley's royalty earnings grew, his self-imposed annual personal budget stayed at 30 pounds, until 98% of his income was given away. He lived up to his promise that "If I leave behind me ten pounds . . . you and all mankind bear witness against me that 'I lived and died a thief and a robber.'" [Harvey, pp. 78, 79]

George Mueller

Because of Mueller's belief that money was a divine stewardship, and therefore should be used under the direction of God Himself, Mueller adopted these four great rules to govern his finances.

- Not to receive any fixed salary.
- Never to ask any human being for help.
- To take this command (Luke 12:33) literally, "Sell that thou hast and give alms," and never to save up money, but to

spend all God entrusted to him on God's poor, on the work of His kingdom.

- Also to take Romans 13:8, "Owe no man anything," literally, and never to buy on credit, or be in debt for anything, but to trust God to provide.

During an interview with Charles Parsons in which Mueller related many of the miraculous answers to prayer he had experienced, he was asked whether he had ever contemplated establishing a reserve fund. He responded:

> To do so would be an act of greatest folly. How could I pray if I had reserves? God would say, "Bring out those reserves, George Mueller." Oh no, I never thought of such a thing. Our reserve fund is in Heaven. The living God is our sufficiency. *I have trusted Him for one dollar; I have trusted Him for thousands, and never trusted in vain.* "Blessed is the man that trusteth in Him." (Psalm 34:8) [Sims, p. 3; emphasis in the original]

Next he was asked whether he had ever thought of saving for himself. In reply, he handed a small purse to Pastor Parsons and said:

> All I am possessed of is in the purse—every penny! Save for myself? Never! When money is sent to me for my own use, I pass it on to God. As much as five thousand dollars has thus been sent at one time, but I do not regard such gifts as belonging to me; they belong to Him, whose I am, and whom I serve. Save for myself? I dare not save; it would dishonor my loving, gracious, all-bountiful Father. [Sims, p. 4]

Anthony Norris Groves

Anthony Groves, a contemporary of George Mueller, was a wealthy dentist who, after becoming convicted about what the Bible says about wealth, sold his possessions, gave away most of the proceeds, and took his family to India as missionaries. The following quotes are from Groves' book *Christian Devotedness:*

> I still believe that He means simply what He says in "Lay not up for yourselves treasures upon earth" etc. There is an eye-salve in this doctrine, when received by faith, that wonderfully clears the field of our spiritual perceptions. [p. 5]

> As to capital and estates, after knowing that our loving Father will supply us in every need, the sooner we are disencumbered by distribution of these for His honor and His service, the better. Then we shall have the happiness of seeing it spent for the glory of him *whose it is,* and for whom we are *only stewards.* Otherwise, if we were to die tomorrow, we do not know whether the capital and estates would fall into the hands of a wise man or a fool. [p. 7, emphasis in the original]

> Can we with any truth be said to love that neighbor as ourselves when we allow him to starve while we have enough and to spare? [p. 26]

> All our misconceptions on this subject seem to arise from one deeply rooted opinion, learnt of Satan and the world over which he presides, that riches and comforts are better for our children than poverty and dependence. The whole tenor of the New Testament, however, pronounces the opinion to be false. [p. 28]

If any object to selling "houses or lands," it remains for them to distinguish between the motives which induce them to retain their property and those which induced the "young man" to retain his. [p. 49]

I shall, therefore, briefly recapitulate the reasons why it appears to me that our Savior spoke literal truth and intended that He should be understood as so speaking when He used such expressions as these, "Lay not up for yourselves treasures upon earth," and "Sell all that thou hast":

1. Because He commanded the young man to do so.
2. Because He commended the poor widow for doing so.
3. Because the apostles and all who believed at Jerusalem did so, by selling their goods, houses, and lands.
4. Because without this dedication, it is impossible to receive the command, "Love thy neighbor as thyself."
5. Because, while obviously it tends to the general extension of Christ's Kingdom upon earth, it does also, in an equal measure, contribute to the happiness and usefulness of the individual, by extirpating carefulness and sloth, and causing to grow in abundance the peaceable fruits of righteousness and love. [pp. 47, 48]

William MacDonald

The following quotes are taken from MacDonald's book *True Discipleship*:

Yet the truth remains that it is *sin* to lay up treasures on earth. It is directly contrary to the Word of God. What we call prudence and foresight is actually rebellion and iniquity. [p. 109, emphasis in the original]

But it is also wrong (to accumulate wealth) because it overlooks the vast spiritual need of the world today. . . . Millions of men and women, boys and girls have never heard the gospel of the grace of God. Millions do not have a Bible, or good gospel literature. Millions are dying without God, without Christ, without hope.

It is a form of spiritual fratricide to have the means of spreading the gospel and not to use them (Ezek. 33:6).

And it testifies loudly to a singular lack of God's love in the heart of the hoarder. For "whoever has this world's goods, and sees his brother in need, and shuts up his heart from him, how does the love of God abide in him?" (1 Jn. 3:17). [p. 111]

It's wrong to stockpile money because it is callous to the enormous physical needs of the world. . . . The rich man in Luke 16 was quite unconcerned about the beggar at his gate. If he had just gone to his window and pulled aside the drape, he would have seen a genuine case of need, a worthy object on which to spend some of his money. But he didn't care.

The world is full of Lazaruses. They are lying at our gates. And Jesus is saying to us, "You shall love your neighbor as yourself" (Mt. 22:39). If we refuse to hear Him now, perhaps one day we will hear Him say to us, "I was hungry and you gave Me no food; I was thirsty and you gave Me no drink. . . . Assuredly, I say to you, inasmuch as you did not do it to one of the least of these, you did not do it to Me (Mt. 25:42, 45). [p. 112]

16

IN OTHER WORDS . . .

I n most cases when an unfamiliar doctrine is being taught, the chances for misunderstanding abound. The following discussion deals with a few of the misunderstandings you likely will face if you begin to teach this doctrine to those who have not yet accepted its message.

What the doctrine of nonaccumulation does not say:

- *It doesn't say we have a right to be lazy.* If that is a problem, it's time to read and obey Proverbs 6:6 and Ephesians 4:28.

- *It doesn't say we have a right to waste money.* Some individuals have been frugally putting money into savings for years under the impression that it was good Christian stewardship to do so. The doctrine of nonaccumulation doesn't release them to go out and squander this hard-earned money on luxurious living. Rather, it calls them to reinvest it in a new place, namely, Heaven.

- *It doesn't say we have a right to be irresponsible with our finances.* If we have made financial commitments, then we need to abide by those commitments. As Christians, we ought to do our very best to pay our bills on time, pay back loans in the manner agreed to, and pay our taxes as the government requires. To do any less would be a disgrace to the body of Christ (see Romans 13:7–8).

- *It doesn't say we have a right to judge others.* We have a duty to preach and practice this doctrine to the best of our ability. But we do not have the right to scrutinize the assets and lifestyles of everyone around us and decide where they fall short in applying this doctrine.

- *It doesn't say we have a right to flaunt our giving.* Jesus clearly told us in Matthew 6:1 not to give alms for the purpose of receiving praise of men. If this is our motivation, He said we will forfeit the reward that God Himself wants to give to us. If we give in secret, however, with no thought of who will notice, then God will reward us openly.

- *It doesn't prohibit the earning of money (even a lot of money).* John Wesley, who strongly believed in the doctrine of nonaccumulation, taught this three-point outline for the management of material things:

  1. Earn all you can (without compromising other duties).
  2. Save all you can (reduce personal spending).
  3. Give all you can (put it to use as soon as possible in Christ's kingdom).

Here is also a list of things that the doctrine of nonaccumulation does teach. Essentially, these are alternative ways to articulate the doctrine itself. Although they are worded differently from the definition of the doctrine given in chapter 2, as you consider these statements, you will realize that they are saying pretty much the same thing.

What the doctrine of nonaccumulation does say:

- *It says we must not make investments on this earth.*

- *It says we must give as much as we can as soon as we can.*

- It says if our needs are being supplied, we must not try to increase the amount of earthly assets we own.

- It says if we own more than we need, we actually are to decrease our earthly assets through our giving.

- It says we should love our neighbors as ourselves (Mt. 22:39).

- It says we should do to others as we would want them to do to us (Lk. 6:31).

- It says we should seek first the kingdom of God (Mt. 6:33).

- It says we cannot have God's love in our hearts if we keep more than we need for ourselves while there are others in this world with less than they need (1 Jn. 3:17).

- It says we are to do good unto all men "as we have opportunity," not less than our opportunity (Gal. 6:10).

17

THE REAL MISTAKE OF THE RICH YOUNG RULER

M ost Christians know the story of the rich young ruler very well. Yet, if you asked them what this man's problem was, most of them would give approximately the same answer. They would shake their heads sadly and reply that this man simply loved his earthly possessions too much.

Although it is certainly true that this man loved his riches too much, he also made another very obvious mistake that most people miss. This mistake in many ways was an even greater mistake than that of valuing earthly possessions too much. It was the mistake of *valuing treasures in Heaven too little.*

You see, Jesus had not said "go throw your money into the sea" just so he could be rid of it. Rather, He told him to give it to the poor. And what would be the result of this action? He would receive, Jesus said, "treasure in Heaven."

In other words, Jesus was presenting this young man with an investment opportunity: an opportunity to exchange treasures on earth for treasures in Heaven. It was an invitation to put his money into an investment that would never be affected by moths, rust, or thieves. This investment would never go down in value despite crashes in the stock market or slumps in the real estate market. This investment would earn an outstanding rate of return (a hundredfold). This investment, unlike normal investments, would not even be taken from him at his date of death. Instead, he would be able to enjoy it for all eternity.

In the world wherein he lived, this young man obviously was a financial genius. His friends probably said that everything he touched turned to gold. In reality, though, his success had not come about by mere chance. It happened, rather, because he had trained himself to recognize a good investment when he saw one.

This young man had become an expert at buying low and selling high. He knew how to spot a bargain that no one else would recognize. He also had learned to know the right time to cut his losses and get out of an investment. Diligent research, consistent self-discipline, and natural ability had given him a position among the financial elite of his time.

To a man so obviously skilled at recognizing value when he saw it, this offer from Jesus should have jumped out as the deal of a lifetime. "What an opportunity!" he should have thought. "I can trade assets that will last several decades (at the most) for assets that will last forever!"

Yet no matter how brilliant he was at picking stocks, playing the futures markets, or snatching up real estate bargains, this man somehow missed seeing the investment opportunity of the century. By simply giving to the poor (in the name of Jesus), he could have gotten in on a deal that would have totally eclipsed the IPOs of Microsoft, Wal-Mart, or General Electric. His net worth would have instantly leapfrogged that of John Rockefeller, Bill Gates, and King Solomon all put together.

Despite his genius in making investment decisions, he somehow overlooked the incredible worth of this deal he was being offered, and he chose to pass it up. Or, as we would say today, he "blew it big time."

Will you and I blow it?

18
AN EXCHANGE OF VALUES

B efore the doctrine of nonaccumulation can take its rightful place in our lives, it must first win the battle against its greatest enemy. This enemy, if not completely destroyed, will become an insurmountable barrier to the acceptance of this doctrine. It doesn't matter how many Scriptures there are to support the doctrine or the number of arguments that exist to prove it to be true, a person will never be able truly to accept this doctrine if this enemy is left standing.

The name of this enemy is "a wrong value system." It is a value system that tells us the things of this world have genuine value (as opposed to being worthless). It tells us that having much of this world's wealth is somehow better than having little of it.

None of us are exempt from the effects of this erroneous value system. All humans are born with it, and it usually becomes evident in children at a very young age. It is what drives people to own, to possess, and to take control over things such as toys, food, money, businesses, and entire nations.

We cannot truly accept the doctrine of nonaccumulation unless we first adopt the value system of Jesus. And we cannot adopt the value system of Jesus unless we give up the value system we received at birth, the value system of this world.

The world says that stocks, bonds, gold coins, land, and savings accounts have real value. Christ says that nothing on earth has any real value except that which can be converted into Heavenly treasure before we die. The world says that financial security is something we all should strive to achieve. Christ says that financial security is something that will destroy our faith and steal our love. The world says that it is honorable to leave your children financially well off. Christ says that such a move would endanger their souls, because a rich person will hardly enter the kingdom of God.

To accept the complete gospel of Jesus Christ, including the doctrine of nonaccumulation, we must exchange our values for His values. In the deepest recesses of our heart, the things that the world considers valuable must be replaced with that which Christ considers valuable.

If you can completely internalize this upside-down value system, it will revolutionize your life. That which you used to think was important will now seem trivial. Your passion will become the kingdom of God. Your thoughts and actions will be centered on eternity, not on this present life.

If this exchange of values does not take place in your heart, however, this book will seem like a legalistic burden or even pure heresy. But once it has happened, everything else this book mentions will seem so obvious to you that writing it down will actually become rather unnecessary.

With this new value system in place, the practical applications I am about to suggest will be things you will naturally want to do, not things you have to do.

19

PRACTICALLY SPEAKING

A lthough the message of this book is primarily doctrinal (what the doctrine of nonaccumulation is and whether or not it is true), we do want to spend a little time discussing some of the practical applications of this doctrine. After all, Jesus' goal in giving us these commands is to change far more than just our *theology*. He wants our *actions* to change as well.

Keep in mind, though, that if you have not yet accepted the doctrine itself as true, nor made the exchange of values described in the preceding chapter, then the suggestions in this chapter will seem legalistic and burdensome to you. If, however, you have made this exchange of values, then you probably have already come to many of the conclusions suggested in this chapter.

As you read these suggestions, keep in mind that they are not Scripture. They are merely suggestions from the author about how you might apply Scripture. Some of you will think that these suggestions are taking this doctrine to the extreme. Others of you will think that I'm not going far enough with these applications.

During a discussion such as this, there are some questions that almost always come up ("Is it wrong to do this?" "Must we do that?" and the like). Most such questions I have purposely avoided answering. These questions usually are evidence that the questioner has not yet accepted the doctrine or the necessary exchange of values. Until that happens, trying to give an answer to such questions would be pointless.

The important thing to remember is that it is Jesus who says "lay not up" and "sell and give," and that these commands therefore have "all authority" behind them. Each of us will bear the ultimate responsibility before God about what it means for us personally to be obedient in these things.

For those of you, then, who have recognized the truth of this doctrine and desire to put it into practice, here are a few suggestions about where you could start.

- *Clean out your retirement account(s),* and give the proceeds to charity. (Yes, you may have to pay some tax to do this, but there should still be a large chunk of it available to donate.) Don't give in to the temptation to dwell on all the wealth that will be "lost" if you do this (you're going to lose it eventually anyway). Think instead about the thousands who will hear the gospel for the first time or receive lifesaving food and medicine because of your action. Then get your Bible and read Matthew 25:31–46.

- *Take an inventory of the rest of your earthly assets to see which of them, if any, could be converted into heavenly treasure.* Which of my assets could be sold, and which could not? Which of them do I really need, and which are simply a luxury?

- *Divide all your assets into two groups: tools versus investments.* A tool's primary purpose is to be used. An investment's primary purpose is to store wealth. (Secondary objectives of an investment are to produce a return on investment and to allow capital appreciation.) Why is this distinction important? Because I believe that, at a minimum, Jesus' command to "sell and give" applies to those assets that qualify as investments.

  This classification may not be immediately apparent, nor will a particular asset always fall into the same category. Owning a piece of farmland, for instance, would probably be an investment for a doctor or a lawyer. For a farmer, however, it could very well be classed as a tool because he can't make a living without it. Owning a house could be a tool for someone who is living in it, but would probably be an investment for someone who is renting it out. Keeping $20,000 of cash in a bank account could be a tool for a business owner who needs to make payroll every two weeks, but would probably be an investment for a day laborer who is just trying to prepare for a "rainy day."

But even these classifications will fall short at times. Farmland could be an investment even for a farmer if he continues to add to the amount of land he owns. Even a house in which you are living could be your investment if your primary motive for owning it is to store wealth or to enjoy capital appreciation. Even an active business could become an investment depending on the scale of operation and the goals for expansion in the future. (Continual expansion is far different from simply operating a business as efficiently as possible, pulling out the profits on a regular basis, and investing those profits in God's kingdom.) Either way, this will be a judgment call you will have to make based on your own lifestyle, your employment situation, and your *motives* for owning the things you do.

- *Give up your financial goals.* If you ask most Christians, "Do you have a desire to be rich?" they would answer with a resounding "no." Here, however, is a much more revealing question. "Do you have a desire to be richer than you are right now?" Or to ask it another way, "Do you hope to own more assets at the end of this year than you did at the end of last year." (If your answer is "yes," are you not in violation of Matthew 6:19? Is not this the very definition of the word "covetousness"?)

  Here is another question. "Would I be disappointed if my assets actually *decreased* from this year to next year?"

  Whatever your financial goals are, give up the ones that make you richer in earthly assets. Develop goals instead that allow you to invest as much as possible in Heavenly treasure, goals that decrease your attachment to this world and increase your dependence on God.

- *Pray this prayer: "Lord, give me enough work for my life, and enough life for my work."* Thousands upon thousands of people have not prayed this prayer, intending rather to retire sometime before their life is finished, only to die shortly before their intended date of retirement. "Then whose shall those things be which thou hast provided?" (Luke 12:20)

- *Explain to your children your convictions regarding finances.* Explain to them that you believe in the doctrine of nonaccumulation, and thus you are not planning to lay anything aside for your old age. Tell them that although you hope to be able to work enough to provide for your own needs right up until the day you die, there may come a day when you can no longer do so. And in that case, according to 1 Timothy 5:8, the primary responsibility for your provision will fall on them. (When this verse speaks of providing for your own, it is referring to taking care of the older generation, not the younger one.)

- *Join a church that teaches and practices the doctrine of nonaccumulation.* (If you can't find such a church, give your pastor a copy of this book.) When the members of an entire church have committed themselves to lay up nothing on earth and everything in Heaven, it is to be expected that there will be some invalids, widows, and elderly who will not have resources of their own or family to take care of them. No one should resent caring for you in your old age if that becomes necessary, because they will very likely be in the same shoes as you some day. In the meantime, do everything in your power to help provide for the needy around you: first your own family members, then fellow Christians, and finally those outside the body of Christ.

- *Go to your parents and tell them that you intend to do all you can to provide for them in their old age.* They should therefore feel the liberty to practice both Matthew 6:19 and Luke 12:33, selling off earthly investments and giving the money to charity.

- *Stretch yourself in your giving.* Make sacrificial choices that allow you to give more. Cut back where you can on your living expenses. Look for ways to increase your earning power. Ask your boss if you can work some extra hours (or else invest these same hours in some sort of kingdom-building ministry). If you haven't been giving at all, start immediately with a tithe (10%), whether you think you can afford it or not. Then, as your earnings go up, increase your giving percentage accordingly.

  Learn as much as you can about a variety of ministries so you can both pray for them and give to them more intelligently. Focus your giving especially on ministries that are most effectively doing the will of the Father, namely, those engaged in *helping the poor* and in *winning the lost* (see Mt. 25:31–46 and Mk. 16:15–16). Keep in mind also that the vast majority of genuine need exists outside of American soil.

- *Practice the "squirrel principle."* A squirrel's "payday" is once a year (the annual nut crop), so he stores enough to get him by until the next one. He doesn't aim to store so much that he won't have to harvest again next year. Following his example, decide what your pay period is and plan accordingly. If you get paid monthly, keep enough from one paycheck to supply your needs until the following one.

Then, if you still have money left over when the next paycheck arrives, give that money to charity and start over.

• *Make a commitment not to increase the assets you own (especially investment type assets) beyond those currently in your possession.* This does not necessarily mean that your income will never increase. Rather, it means that if your income does go up, your giving will go up at the same rate: "as God hath prospered him" (1 Cor. 16:2).

• *Find a replacement passion.* Whether you like to admit it or not, if you have been accumulating wealth on this earth, that activity has been filling an emotional need in your life. It will be almost impossible to quit "cold turkey" without taking up some other activity to fulfill that need.

Get actively involved in something of eternal value, such as prison ministry, tract distribution, or intercessory prayer. Or perhaps God simply wants you to take up a ministry of giving to others who are involved in these things. Whatever it is that God is calling you to, put your all into it. In other words, make it your passion.

20

THE WITNESSES

I magine this scene.

It is Judgment Day, and from way back in the line of all the world's billions, you see Jesus sitting on the throne of His glory, dividing the people into two groups, "as a shepherd divides his sheep from the goats."

The news soon makes its way back to you that the criterion for this division is the question of whether or not we have fed the hungry, clothed the naked, taken in strangers, and so on. "Because," says the King, "inasmuch as ye have done it unto one of the least of these my brethren, ye have done it unto me."

As your turn for judgment draws near, you wonder what your fate will be. You do not have long to wait. You are soon standing before the Almighty Judge, waiting to see whether you have succeeded or failed in obeying the mandate, "As we have therefore opportunity, let us do good unto all men . . ."

"Call the witnesses," orders the bailiff. "Witnesses?" you wonder to yourself. "I didn't know there were going to be witnesses."

But yes, there will be witnesses, two groups of them, in fact. The first group to enter the courtroom are the widows, the orphans, and the beggars who had lived and died (or more specifically, starved to death) during your lifetime. These people had all lived within reach of any help you would have wanted to offer them. Some could have been reached by you in person; others you could have aided by means of a charitable organization.

"Call the next witnesses," comes the order again from the bailiff. You wonder with a growing apprehension who these witnesses could possibly be.

And then you see them. A door opens, and out come all the stocks, bonds, gold coins, rental property, and retirement accounts that you had invested in while on earth. You had chosen to hold on to these items for you own security rather than giving them up for the needs around you. Together, all these assets turn and point one big accusing finger—at you. The verdict is clear. You have nowhere to hide. You bow your head in utter shame and despair.

Go to now, ye rich men, weep and howl for your miseries that shall come upon you. Your riches are corrupted, and your garments are motheaten. Your gold and silver is cankered; and *the rust of them shall be a witness against you*, and shall eat your flesh as it were fire. Ye have heaped treasure together for the last days (Jas. 5:1–3).

I would be afraid to keep a live cobra in my house. I would be afraid to keep a ticking time bomb under my bed. I would be afraid to keep an open bottle of poison within reach of my children.

But I would be absolutely terrified, after reading James 5:1–3, to keep for myself a large store of earthly investments as long as there are still hungry people in this world.

21

FRANK, THE WISE INVESTOR

The following story is an imaginary account about a man who was a wise investor by this world's standards. If the financial experts of our time read this story, they all would agree that this man certainly knew what he was doing when it came to investing on this earth. They would lift him up as a prime example of how a man who starts out with virtually nothing can still, through patience, hard work, and wise investment decisions, develop for himself a fortune worth millions.

Jesus was burdened that his people also make wise investment decisions. We ought therefore to follow this man's example in many ways. The main difference is that whereas this man was a citizen of the United States, we are called to be citizens of God's kingdom. This man's actions, therefore, must be altered accordingly before we put them to practice in our lives.

As a backdrop for this story, we have used the true account of one of the most profitable companies that has ever been traded in the stock market: Microsoft Corporation. In 1986 this company went public, offering its stock for sale at an initial price of less than $25 per share. Since that time, Microsoft has grown to the point that one of these same shares would now be worth nearly 300 times that amount. This growth has catapulted Microsoft's founder, Bill Gates, to the top of the list of the richest men on earth, with a net worth of more than $40 billion.

In early 1986, a man whom we'll call Frank walked into the office of an investment advisor and sat down for an interview. He explained to the advisor both his current financial situation and his financial goals for the future. Although he was not a rich man, Frank said he did have several thousand dollars in a savings account. More importantly, he had a young body, a sharp mind, a well-paying job, and a willingness to put everything he had into his goal of becoming financially wealthy.

After looking at Frank's situation, the advisor explained to Frank some of the risks and rewards of investing in the stock market and suggested that because of his young age and long-term goals, he should consider putting at least some of his money into this type of investment. He also cautioned Frank never to invest in a company without researching it thoroughly. He then gave Frank a few pointers on how to analyze a company's long-term prospects.

Before Frank walked out the door, the advisor made this comment, "One stock you might want to consider, Frank, is a company that is going to go public next month. Its name is Microsoft, and it seems to be a company with a really good growth potential. Just make sure you do your own research on the company before you make your final decision."

Over the next few weeks, Frank did do a lot of research on this company named Microsoft, even getting a chance to interview the president, Bill Gates himself. After coming out of that meeting, Frank was absolutely convinced that Microsoft was the best investment opportunity ever offered in the financial world.

Frank did not waste any time in taking action on this conviction. Upon arriving at home, he called his bank and ordered it to take every penny from his savings account and put it into Microsoft stock. Next, he went through his other belongings to see what else he could do to free up more money to invest. To start with, he decided to sell his coin collection that had been gathering dust in the back closet. Then he took his three guns to a sporting goods store and negotiated a sale price for them. Next, he drove his late-model car to a local dealer and exchanged it for a less expensive model, walking away with $2,000 cash in his pocket. Finally, he took all the money produced by these efforts and sent it straight to his broker to be invested in Microsoft.

Frank's next move was to call the administrator of the retirement plan offered by his employer. Frank had been contributing to this plan through automatic withdrawals from his weekly paycheck, and the balance by now had grown to slightly more than $4,000. He asked the administrator whether Microsoft stock was one of the investment options offered by this plan. When he was told that it was not, Frank decided to withdraw all his money from the plan and invest it in Microsoft. His tax accountant warned him sternly that this withdrawal would cost him both income tax and a 10% penalty on the amount withdrawn. Frank, however, decided to do it anyway. He was convinced that the growth potential of Microsoft was enough to easily offset any additional tax that he would have to pay. As a result, Frank was able to add almost $3,000 to his total holdings in Microsoft stock.

After arriving at work the next day, Frank asked his boss for permission to work several extra hours of overtime each week. The boss granted his request, and from then on the extra income generated by this work was invested directly into Microsoft stock.

Frank also began to live more frugally, limiting his personal spending as much as possible. He started buying less expensive clothes, went out to eat less often, and took fewer and simpler vacations. This lifestyle freed up even more money to be invested in Microsoft. Any spare time he did have was spent reading, thinking, and talking about Microsoft Corporation. It had become a passion that consumed every aspect of his life.

One day Frank received a call from the personnel director of Microsoft. He was told that during his interview with Bill Gates several weeks earlier, Gates had been so impressed with him that he was inviting him to come and work for Microsoft. The director offered Frank a salary more than double the wage he was currently earning, and Frank quickly accepted.

Over the next several months, Frank put all his effort into his job at Microsoft, working his way up through several management levels as he learned more and more about the company. As his earnings continued to increase, he continued to invest everything above his basic living expenses directly into Microsoft stock. Because of his increased income, he was now able to put well over half of his monthly paycheck into this investment, and his total holdings were accumulating rapidly.

After some time had passed, an even more exciting opportunity presented itself. Frank was called into the office of Bill Gates himself, and the president had this request for him. "Frank, I'd like you to move to Russia for ten years to become the representative for Microsoft in that country. I realize that there is a lot of inconvenience involved in moving to and living in a foreign country, and for that reason I'm offering to give you a salary three times the amount you are currently making.

"I have just one caution for you," Bill continued, "Do not make any investments in Russia while you are there. The political situation in Russia is on very shaky ground, and the communists could take over the country at any time. If that should happen, everything you own would immediately pass into their hands. The only safe option is to send your money over here to America and let me invest it in Microsoft for you.

"Furthermore," Bill continued, "I have another reason why I don't want you to make investments in Russia. After ten years I want you to return home to work for me here. If you start making investments in the country of Russia, you will become so attached to that country that you won't want to leave when the time comes. So please send everything you make back here to America so you don't lose sight of the fact that you are only in that country temporarily, and that very soon your sojourn there will be over."

Frank decided to accept the offer, knowing that the increased income would provide a huge boost toward his goal of becoming financially wealthy. After arriving in Russia, he found a modest house to rent, purchased a small car to drive, and began putting all his effort into working for Microsoft's branch office in Russia. And always, after picking up his paycheck every month, he would take out what he needed for living expenses and send the balance to America to be invested in Microsoft.

As time went on, Frank's Russian landlord decided to sell the house where Frank was living, and he needed to find another place to live. But suddenly, it seemed that there simply were no other houses around to rent; his only option was to buy a place of his own. Inexpensive houses were readily available, and Frank soon found and bought one that met his needs. Although this purchase caused a temporary decrease in the flow of money he was sending back to America, it seemed to be his only option at the time.

More time passed, and the area where Frank was living experienced a tremendous boom in the real estate market. The little house Frank had bought for only $60,000 soon became worth nearly $250,000. As Frank thought about this turn of events, and about his newfound Russian wealth, he recalled the warning that Bill Gates had given him before he left America: "Don't make investments in the country of Russia." Frank began to wonder whether there would be any way to move this $250,000 of equity to a more secure location rather than leave it to the mercy of Russia's unstable economy.

The answer to this dilemma came one day when Frank was visiting with his next-door neighbor, a lifelong citizen of Russia. When the neighbor mentioned that he would be interested in investing in a piece of rental real estate, Frank's ears immediately perked up. "Would you like to buy my house, and then rent it back to me?" he asked his neighbor. The neighbor was very interested in such an arrangement, and the deal was made within a week. After paying for the closing costs, Frank walked away with well over $200,000 in his pocket, which he immediately converted into American dollars and sent across the ocean to be invested in Microsoft stock.

At various times during his stay in Russia, Frank was approached by his neighbors and coworkers, who recommended different investment opportunities to him. Sometimes they recommended a piece of land. Other times it was a company on the Russian stock market, and still other times people told him about the great interest rate he could earn at a particular Russian bank. Frank always tried to explain to them why he wasn't interested. He told them of the dangers associated with investing in Russia. He told them of the far more wonderful investment opportunities to which he already had access. And he explained to them that it would be foolish for him to forego even a little of his investment opportunity in America to invest in anything that Russia had to offer.

At other times, his Russian friends encouraged him to try to enjoy life a little more during his stay in their country. They told him of the wonderful restaurants, vacation resorts, and amusement parks within driving distance. With the large amount of money he was earning each month, they told him, he could be having a grand time while living in Russia. But again, Frank explained that he had not come to Russia to have a good time, but rather to accumulate as much wealth as possible in a company called Microsoft in that faraway land called America.

The response from his Russian friends was usually the same. They looked at him with a mixture of disbelief and pity, as though he were some sort of lunatic. Why should he be putting all of his hard-earned money into this company that he could not even see? And after all these years, how could he even be sure there really even was such a place as America?

A number of times during his Russian sojourn Frank was pleasantly surprised by some extra money coming his way. Several times he received income tax refunds far greater than he had been expecting. Another time he received an inheritance check from a relative he hardly knew. But no matter where the money came from, his response was always the same: convert it to American dollars and send it across the ocean to be invested in Microsoft. Although he was tempted at times to use these extra funds either to raise his standard of living or to store up some reserves right there in Russia, he did his best to resist these temptations and to look forward to the day when he would be going home for good.

It would have been nice if Frank had experienced nothing but financial prosperity during the time he was in Russia, but this was not the case. He also experienced some significant financial setbacks during his stay there. In one case, for instance, he had to have emergency surgery, which would cost him well over $50,000. How in the world was he going to handle this? The doctors performing the surgery wanted to be paid right away, but Frank did not have anywhere near that amount of money, having sent all his extra income to America. Had Frank made a mistake by not keeping a reserve fund in Russia for situations such as this?

The solution was simple. Frank placed a collect call to Bill Gates and told him of the dilemma. Bill told him not to worry. The money would be wired over to him yet that day. "And, oh, by the way, Frank," Bill told him, "don't worry about this withdrawal depleting the value of your investment in Microsoft. Your account is so large by this time that this really won't even make much of a dent in it."

This last comment set Frank's mind to wondering: how much was his investment worth by this time? He hadn't been able to keep very close track. The communication system between the two countries was a little like seeing "through a glass, darkly." He had believed from the beginning that Microsoft was a good company and, because of that belief, had entrusted them with everything he owned. But every once in a while a small doubt would arise in his mind about whether all his effort would really be worthwhile in the long run.

The day finally came when Bill's predictions came true. Russia's economy collapsed. The communists took control of the country, and all private property passed into the hands of the government. Frank was able to get on a last-minute flight out of the country, carrying nothing but the shirt on his back.

As he sat thinking on his long flight across the Atlantic, Frank began to ponder all that had transpired. His first thought was one of gratitude to Bill for the wise counsel he had given. Most of Frank's Russian friends had lost everything they owned in a matter of hours. All they had ever lived for had been suddenly snatched from their hands with no time to prepare. Frank, on the other hand, had lost virtually nothing in the revolution. Even the equity in his personal residence had been moved to safety ahead of time.

Next he began to wonder: What will happen to me when I land in New York? Will anyone be there to meet me? Will I have a place to live and food to eat? Have my investments really done as well as Bill says they have? Or will I be a penniless pauper wondering the streets looking for work? The same old nagging doubts were just enough to give him a slight feeling of uneasiness as the plane began its final descent toward American soil.

As Frank walked down the ramp into the airport terminal, he noticed a large group of important-looking people who appeared to be waiting expectantly for someone. It wasn't until he saw Bill Gates himself at the head of the procession and the huge banner reading "Welcome Home, Frank" that he realized all these people were waiting for *him!* There were newspaper reporters, cameramen, a television station, and all the top people in Microsoft, all gathered there, they said, to give a royal welcome to *one of the richest men in America!*

Yes, it was true, Bill explained to Frank as they headed through the terminal. Microsoft's astounding growth and Frank's diligent investing had combined to make him one of the wealthiest men in America. With this kind of wealth, Bill told him, he could enjoy the very best of everything America had to offer. A lack of money would never be a problem for him again as long as he lived.

As the story of Frank's Russian sojourn, his investment habits, and his astounding wealth made headlines across the country, different people had different reactions. Some were jealous of him. Others resolved to imitate him. Some simply sat back and admired him. But there was one thing everybody was forced to admit without any reservations: Frank had been a very, very wise investor.

22

FINALLY, BRETHREN

I'm sure as you read the story of the wise investor named Frank, you were able to discern the parallels between his situation in Russia and ours on this earth.

- Like Frank, we are living as pilgrims and strangers in a foreign country.
- Like Frank, we have been commanded not to make investments in the country where we are living.
- Like Frank, we are encouraged to invest everything that we can in our homeland.
- Like Frank, commitment to these investment principles brings us ridicule from those who have not made such a commitment.
- Like Frank, if we are faithful to invest in our homeland and to avoid foreign investing, it will have a great impact on our future welfare.
- Like Frank, we prove which kingdom we are truly trusting in by the place where we make our investments.
- Like Frank, we have no good reason to store up wealth in the country where we are temporarily living because our God has promised to supply our need.

So is the doctrine of nonaccumulation a true doctrine? Have you (or has your church) accepted this doctrine as true? Are you willing to commit yourself to "do and teach" this doctrine along with the rest of Christ's Sermon on the Mount?

By the way, if you believe (as I do) that the Sermon on the Mount is for us today, and that we should obey its teaching on divorce and remarriage, nonswearing of oaths, and nonresistance, then it seems only to make sense to believe in nonaccumulation also. It just isn't consistent to accept *part* of the Sermon on the Mount, such as nonresistance, without also accepting its teaching about nonaccumulation.

If nonresistance is meant to be practiced today, then so is nonaccumulation. If nonaccumulation doesn't apply to us, however, then neither does nonresistance. Both of these doctrines are key parts of Christ's Sermon on the Mount. Both are given to us as commandments to obey. Both are part of the teachings of the "kingdom of God" that Jesus preached everywhere he went.

I will speak for myself. I believe the doctrine of nonaccumulation is a true doctrine. If someone were to ask me to describe my (strange) views on the subject of economics, that is how I would answer them (that I believe in the doctrine of nonaccumulation). This answer would doubtless lead to more questions, which hopefully would give me the opportunity to explain what it is that this doctrine teaches.

I desire, however, to do more than just believe this doctrine. My goal is also to put it into practice as God leads. And although I have already taken certain actions and made certain commitments with that goal in mind, I have also read numerous testimonies of other Christians who have put this doctrine into practice to a far greater degree than I have. But rather than try to explain away the actions of these Christians as something extreme or unnecessary, I will instead allow their testimonies to challenge me more and more to a life of faith.

This doctrine stands on its own, whether I personally obey it perfectly or not. It will challenge me continually until the day I die, and prompt me to say, with Paul,

> Not as though I had already attained, either were already perfect: but I follow after, if that I may apprehend that for which also I am apprehended of Christ Jesus. Brethren, I count not myself to have apprehended: but this one thing I

do, forgetting those things which are behind, and reaching forth unto those things which are before, I press toward the mark for the prize of the high calling of God in Christ Jesus (Phil. 3:12–14).

Do you have questions or comments about this book? If so, I'd love to hear from you.

Roger Hertzler
27027 Irish Bend Loop
Halsey, OR 97348

Email: rogerhertzler@afo.net

Appendix

The Commands of Christ on the Use of Possessions

Maybe you feel that this book has been dominated by man's opinion rather than by what the Bible really says. Just in case that is true, I've included this Appendix, made up almost entirely of New Testament verses that deal with the subject of economics. If you decide to throw away the rest of this book, go ahead, but first tear out this chapter and keep it. After all, you are already carrying around these same passages with you if you have a complete New Testament.

What are Christ's commands?

1. Matthew 6:19a

- "Lay not up for yourselves treasures upon earth." (*KJV*)
- "Do not store up for yourselves treasures on earth." (*NASB*)
- "Make no store of wealth for yourselves on earth." (*Bible in Basic English*)

  1a. This night thy soul shall be required of thee: then whose shall those things be? So is he that layeth up treasure for himself. (Lk. 12:20–21)

  1b. Take therefore no thought for the morrow. (Mt. 6:34)

  1c. Beware of covetousness, for a man's life consisteth not in the abundance of things which he possesseth. (Lk. 12:15)

  1d. They that will be rich fall into temptation and a snare . . . but thou, O man of God, flee these things. (1 Tim. 6:9, 11)

  1e. Keep your lives free from the love of money, and be content with what you have. (Heb. 13:5)

1f. Covetousness, let it not be once named among you. (Eph. 5:3)

1g. But seek ye first the kingdom of God. (Mt. 6:33)

2. Luke 12:33a

- "Sell that ye have, and give alms." *(KJV)*
- "Sell your possessions, and give to charity." *(NASB)*
- "Give what property you have in exchange for money, and give the money to the poor." *(Bible in Basic English)*

2a. But lay up for yourselves treasures in Heaven. (Mt. 6:20)

2b. Give to every man that asketh thee. (Lk. 6:30)

2c. And if any man sue thee at the law, and take away thy coat, let him have thy cloak also. (Mt. 5:40)

2d. Lend, hoping for nothing again. (Lk. 6:35)

2e. Use worldly wealth to gain friends for yourselves. (Lk. 16:9)

2f. As ye would that men should do to you, do ye even so to them. (Lk. 6:31)

2g. But rather give alms of such things as ye have. (Lk. 11:41)

What are the principles behind Christ's commands?

1. Where your treasure is, there will your heart be also. (Mt. 6:21)
2. Ye cannot serve God and mammon. (Lk. 16:13)
3. For that which is highly esteemed among men is abomination in the sight of God. (Lk. 16:15)
4. The love of money is the root of all evil. (1 Tim. 6:10)
5. He hath anointed me to preach the gospel to the poor. (Lk. 4:18)
6. Blessed are you who are poor. (Lk. 6:20)
7. Hath not God chosen the poor of this world rich in faith, and heirs of the kingdom? (Jas. 2:5)
8. And the rich he hath sent empty away. (Lk. 1:53)

9. But woe unto you that are rich. (Lk. 6:24)
10. It is easier for a camel to go through the eye of a needle, than for a rich man to enter into the kingdom of God. (Mt. 19:24)
11. Whosoever he be of you that forsaketh not all that he hath, he cannot be my disciple. (Lk. 14:33)
12. If anyone has material possessions and sees his brother in need but has no pity on him, how can the love of God be in him? (1 Jn. 3:17)
13. Inasmuch as ye have done it unto one of the least of these my brethren, ye have done it unto me. (Mt. 25:40)
14. My God shall supply all your need. (Phil. 4:19)

How important is it to obey Christ's commands?

1. Ye are my friends, if ye do whatsoever I command you. (Jn. 15:14)
2. And every one that heareth these sayings of mine, and doeth them not, shall be likened unto a foolish man. (Mt. 7:24)
3. Why call ye me, Lord, Lord, and do not the things which I say? (Lk. 6:46)
4. And hereby do we know that we know him, if we keep his commandments. He that saith, I know him, and keepeth not his commandments, is a liar, and the truth is not in him. (1 Jn. 2:3–4)
5. He that hath my commandments, and keepeth them, he it is that loveth me. (Jn. 14:21)
6. In flaming fire taking vengeance on them that . . . obey not the gospel of our Lord Jesus Christ. (2 Thess. 1:8)
7. If ye love me, keep my commandments. (Jn. 14:15)
8. Not every one that saith unto me, Lord, Lord, shall enter into the kingdom of heaven; but he that doeth the will of my Father which is in heaven. (Mt. 7:21)

What classes of people should obey Christ's commands?

1. Charge them that are rich . . . that they be . . . ready to distribute. (1 Tim. 6:17–18)
2. Yet lackest thou one thing: sell all that thou hast, and distribute unto the poor . . . he was very rich. (Lk. 18:22–23)
3. Zacchaeus . . . he was rich . . . and said . . . the half of my goods I give to the poor. (Lk. 19:2, 8)
4. This poor widow hath cast in more than they all. (Lk. 21:3)
5. He that hath two coats, let him impart to him that hath none. (Lk. 3:11)
6. In . . . their deep poverty . . . beyond their power . . . gave. (2 Cor. 8:2, 3, 5)
7. Let him that stole steal no more: but rather let him labor, working . . . that he may have to give to him that needeth. (Eph. 4:28)

To what extent should we obey Christ's commands?

1. For if there be first a willing mind, it is accepted according to that a man hath, and not according to that he hath not. (2 Cor. 8:12)
2. That your abundance may be a supply for their want . . . that there may be equality. (2 Cor. 8:14)
3. And sold their possessions and goods, and parted them to all men, as every man had need. (Acts 2:45)
4. Neither was there any among them that lacked: for as many as were possessors of lands or houses sold them . . . and distribution was made unto every man, according as he had need. (Acts 4:34–35)

5. For ye know the grace of our Lord Jesus Christ, that, though he was rich, yet for your sakes He became poor. (2 Cor. 8:9)

6. And having food and raiment, let us be therewith content. (1 Tim. 6:8)

7. As we have therefore opportunity, let us do good unto all men. (Gal. 6:10)

8. Every man according as he purposeth in his heart, so let him give; not grudgingly, or of necessity: for God loveth a cheerful giver. (2 Cor. 9:7)

What are the consequences for not obeying Christ's commands?

1. Go to now, ye rich men, weep and howl for your miseries that shall come upon you. Your riches . . . shall eat at your flesh as it were fire. Ye have heaped treasure together for the last days. (Jas. 5:1–3)

2. Thou in thy lifetime receivedst thy good things, and likewise Lazarus evil things: but now he is comforted, and thou art tormented. (Lk. 16:25)

3. The deceitfulness of riches . . . choke the word, and it becometh unfruitful. (Mk. 4:19)

4. Every branch in me that beareth not fruit he taketh away. (Jn. 15:2)

5. Every tree therefore which bringeth not forth good fruit is hewn down, and cast into the fire. (Lk. 3:9)

6. So then because thou art lukewarm, and neither cold nor hot, I will spue thee out of my mouth. Because thou sayest, I am rich, and increased with goods, and have need of nothing. (Rev. 3:16–17)

7. Depart from me, ye cursed, into everlasting fire . . . for I was an hungered, and ye gave me no meat. (Mt. 25:41–42)

8. And that servant, which knew his lord's will, . . . neither did according to his will, shall be beaten with many stripes. (Lk. 12:47)

Sources

Bercot, David. A *Dictionary of Early Christian Beliefs*. Peabody, Mass.: Hendrickson Publishers, Inc., 1998. Quotations used by permission.

Bercot, David. *The Kingdom That Turned the World Upside Down*. Amberson, Pa.: Scroll Publishing Co., 2003. Quotations used by permission.

Groves, A. N. *Christian Devotedness*. Kansas City: Walterick Publishing Ministries, 2006. Quotations used by permission.

Harvey, Lillian G. *Covetousness (The Sin Very Few Ever Confess)*. Hampton, Tenn.: Harvey Christian Publishers, 2001.

Horsch, John. *Mennonites in Europe*. Scottdale, Pa.: Mennonite Publishing House, 1942.

Kauffman, Daniel, editor. *Doctrines of the Bible*. Scottdale, Pa.: Mennonite Publishing House, 1928.

MacDonald, William. *True Discipleship*. Port Colborne, Ont.: Gospel Folio Press, 2003. Quotations used by permission.

Murray, Andrew. "George Mueller and the Secret of His Power in Prayer," in Andrew Murray, *With Christ in the School of Prayer*. New York: Grosset & Dunlap, n.d.

Simons, Menno. *The Complete Works of Menno Simons*. Elkhart, Ind.: John F. Funk & Bro., 1871.

Sims, A. *An Hour with George Mueller, the Man of Faith to Whom God Gave Millions*. Pensacola, Fl.; Mount Zion Publications, n.d.

Snyder, C. Arnold, editor. *Sources of South German/Austrian Anabaptism*. Kitchener, Ont.: Pandora Press, 2001.

Stutzman, David J., editor. *The Language of the Deathbed*. Millersburg, Oh.: Stutzman Family Books, 1992. Quotations used by permission.

van Braght, Thieleman J., editor. *Martyrs Mirror*. Scottdale, Pa.: Herald Press, 1950.

Yoder, John H. *The Legacy of Michael Sattler*. Scottdale, Pa.: Herald Press, 1973.

As a companion to *Through the Eye of a Needle*, we recommend:

The Gospel of Jesus About The Poor

Jesus calls us to evangelize and make disciples from all nations. But Jesus also commands us to care for the poor. Although many Bible-believing Christians are obedient to Jesus' call to spread the Word, they all too often forget about His gospel concerning the poor. This is sad, because Jesus made it clear that caring for the poor is a salvation issue (Matt. 25)—not something that is optional. A challenging message by David Bercot.

70 min. audio CD $4.95

Available from

Scroll Publishing Co.
P. O. Box 122
Amberson, PA 17210
(717) 349-7033